THE WORLD ACCORDING TO ME

THE WORLD ACCORDING TO ME

RECOGNIZING AND RELEASING OUR ILLUSIONS OF CONTROL

SANDRA D. WILSON, PH.D.

VICTOR BOOKS

A DIVISION OF SCRIPTURE PRESS PUBLICATIONS INC.
USA CANADA ENGLAND

Unless otherwise noted, Scripture quotations are from the *New American Standard Bible,* © the Lockman Foundation 1960, 1962, 1963, 1968, 1971, 1972, 1973, 1975, 1977. Quotations marked KJV are from the *Authorized (King James) Version.* Quotations marked NIV are from *Holy Bible, New International* Version®. Copyright © 1973, 1978, 1984 by International Bible Society. Used by permission of Zondervan Publishing House. All rights reserved.

Editor: Afton Rorvik
Designer: Grace K. Chan Mallette
Cover Photo/Illustration: Grace K. Chan Mallette and Andrea Boven

---

Library of Congress Cataloging-in-Publication Data

Wilson, Sandra D., 1938–
    The world according to me / Sandra D. Wilson.
        p. cm.
    ISBN: 1-56476-487-7
    1. Control (Psychology) — Religious aspects — Christianity. 2. Magical thinking. 3. Spiritual life — Christianity. 4. Emotional maturity — Religious aspects — Christianity. I. Title.
BV4597.53.C62W55   1995
248.4 – dc20   95-16083
                                                                                   CIP

---

1 2 3 4 5 6 7 8 9 10   Printing/Year   99 98 97 96 95

CONTENTS

Introduction   7

PART ONE:
We Long to Control Our World

1   Understanding Personal Power   15
2   Prolonged Magical Thinking and Illusions of Control   26
3   Recognizing Illusions and Illusionists   41

PART TWO:
How Do We Release Control of Our World?

4   Surrendering Our Illusions of Control   53
5   Magical Fixes, Change, and Counseling   67

PART THREE:
Letting Go of Our World, Piece by Piece

6   Illusions of Control, Shame, and Perfectionism   81
7   Illusions of Control in Managing Our Emotions   96
8   Illusions of Control in Relationships   109
9   Illusions of Control within Families   124
10   Illusions of Control and Fairy-tale Faith   139
11   Illusions of Control and Forgiveness   153
12   Illusions of Control versus the Reality of Hope   167

Notes   175

ACKNOWLEDGMENTS

Thank you to Duncan Jaenicke for believing that I was the right person to do this book. Although I've discussed magical thinking's illusions of control in each of my previous books, I had not thought of expanding this topic into an entire volume. Fortunately, Duncan did.

Thank you to Greg Clouse, Afton Rorvik, Pam Campbell, and all the other nice folks at Victor Books for making my maiden voyage with you an enjoyable trip.

Thank you to dear friends and courageous counselees for sharing yourselves and your struggles with control fantasies. It's nice to know that I'm not the only one!

Thank you to my wonderful husband, Garth, for consistently encouraging me as I do the difficult, solitary work of writing.

Above all, I thank God for redeeming me by His grace and for patiently teaching me to trust Him to control my past, my present, and my future.

INTRODUCTION

Have you ever visited The Magic Kingdom? Since Disney World didn't open until I was already an adult, I missed it as a kid. But I got to share the excitement when my husband and I took our children. What a thrill!

In a sense, *all* of us have visited The Magic Kingdom. As young children, without realizing what we were doing, we used a magical kind of thinking and a fairy-tale logic to make sense of the world around us. This childish perception of reality enthrones each of us at the center of our personal universe with unlimited magical power to control people and cause events.

If our families were reasonably healthy, we outgrew this thinking style as we began to experience the realistic limitations of our "magical" powers. Unfortunately, all families are *not* reasonably healthy. This means that many of us, without recognizing it, probably still operate by magical thinking in some aspects of our lives.

I've become a pretty skillful magician over the years. How about you? Oh, I don't mean I bought a magic kit or took lessons from a professional. No, I just practiced the premise of all magical performances—creating illusions that distort reality. And that premise states the means and end of all magical thinking.

Child development specialists universally agree on the existence of infantile grandiosity, more commonly known as magical thinking. However, most adults, including Christians, understand little of the origins, purposes, and effects of magical thinking's illusions of control. In the following pages, you will find practical, understandable ways to recognize magical thinking. You'll also discover motivating hope and clear guidelines to help you substantially relinquish magical thinking for its biblical alternative: faith in the character of God, in the finished work of Jesus Christ, and in the power of the Holy Spirit.

To take this topic seriously, we need to recognize magical thinking's control fantasies in our belief systems and living patterns. But that can be tough. As usual, we recognize unhealthy traits in others far more readily than in ourselves. Here are a few examples of folks who live, to some extent, by magical thinking:

- successful professionals who continually overwork to the point of sacrificing their marriages and families, even their own health, because they hope to win their supervisors' (and maybe their parents') approval;
- incest or rape survivors who wear baggy clothes (or significantly overeat) to hide their bodies' shapeliness because they still believe their perpetrators who said (or implied), "It's your fault for looking that way";
- devout Christians who resent God for letting them or their children get seriously ill after all the years of faithful service they have performed;
- millions of consumers who buy certain toothpastes, perfumes or aftershaves because they believe these products provide some control over others' romantic desires.

The examples go on and on, and as I've admitted, you'll find me in that endless parade.

I've spent most of my adult life, in effect, waving a magic wand. My magical thinking focused on performing and pleasing perfectly enough to control other people's opinions of me and desire to be with me. I also waved that invisible wand in my husband's and children's directions a time or ten by attempting to control and change them.

You've already spotted a theme here, haven't you? The big C word—**CONTROL.** Through my experiences as a counselor, seminary professor, and conference speaker, I've discovered that I'm not the only person on this planet who struggles with the compulsion to contol. This might even be an issue in *your* life. Occassionally.

I wrote this book for all of us who want to learn how and why control-propelled magical thinking invades every aspect of our lives. Chapter 1 lays a foundation for our probe into the mysteries of magical thinking by looking at appropriate and inappropriate uses of personal power. "Why?" takes center stage in chapter 2 where we examine the origins of unhealthy and prolonged magical thinking. Chapter

3 addresses how we recognize illusions in our adult lives. We turn to "what to do about it" in chapter 4 as we face the paradox of conquering our control compulsions by surrendering our magic wands.

Chapters 5–11 discuss major arenas of living often contaminated by prolonged magical thinking. Some of these are personal arenas, such as self-concepts and our emotions. Others are relational arenas, such as friendships and family relationships. When we think magically, our spiritual arena contains what I call fairy-tale faith. We'll look closely at this counterfeit version of genuine biblical believing as it appears both in the so-called "health and wealth" movement and also within conservative evangelical Christianity. Personal, relational, and spiritual arenas converge when we come to the crucial topic of forgiveness. On each of these subjects, I offer practical suggestions for changing our *illusion*-based beliefs and behaviors.

Of course, our overused, wand-waving arms must get painfully tired before we become desperate enough to seriously consider changing. And by the time we come to the end of all our own controlling illusions, we often come to the end of all hope. That's why the last chapter clearly contrasts the magical thinking we need to surrender with the "living hope" we must nurture and cherish. (See 1 Peter 1:3.)

Before you begin this adventure into recognizing and releasing illusions of control, I have two specific suggestions.

ONE
Take time to reflect on the patterns of your life and record what you find.

If you've never done anything like this before, you will likely feel very strange, even selfish, scheduling regular time for personal reflection. As Christians, we may worry that this could make us sinfully self-absorbed. In Proverbs 14:8, God says He wants us to understand the patterns of our lives, called our "ways," rather than to traffic in deceit. With our human propensity for self-deception, we will need more than personal reflection alone to gain this understanding God desires for us. But this lifestyle inventory plays an important part in the process.

To help you begin or move along in your process, I've included a brief **Think about It** section at the end of each chapter. As you read, you may also want to use your personal journal to record information and insights that seem to speak directly to you.

TWO

Ask God to guide and empower you as you begin to practice new, truth-based choices.

Through repeated trial and a lot of error, I've learned something about change that many others learned before me. While we facilitate our changing processes by increasing our understanding, we don't significantly change without making and practicing new choices about how to think and behave. *And I really hate that!* After all, I'm so good at acquiring more and more information and gaining deeper and deeper understanding. I'm not nearly as good at consistently practicing healthy, biblical behaviors.

Does any of this sound familiar? If so, you'll recognize the absolute necessity of relying on God's guidance and power. We just can't pull off this change thing by ourselves. God did not design you or me to be a Lone-Ranger Changer.

We play a part in each other's changing adventures as we pray for each other and as we "speak the truth in love"[1] to encourage, support, and sometimes confront one another when our choices are harmful and unbiblical. By the way, those are all things a good Christian therapist or pastoral counselor does.

I don't think everyone needs a professional counselor. However, some of us may, especially if our belief systems are clogged with a lot of lies we learned by being neglected or abused as children. Sadly, one of those lies may say, "Only weak people ask for help." Recognizing when we need help reflects wisdom, not weakness in my opinion.

God often graciously elects to involve human helpers in His life-changing work, just as Jesus did when He raised Lazarus. When Jesus asked bystanders to roll away the stone blocking Lazarus' grave or unwind his gravecloths, clearly the issue wasn't one of Jesus' sufficiency. Jesus simply used many ways to express His power and work out His purposes in people's lives.

I think Jesus' ways can include having us meet with a wise pastor or biblically-informed counselor, or even read scripturally-based books intended to help us learn more about ourselves and more about Him.

Since this is one of those books, I've asked Jesus to use it to bring insight and blessing into your life.

PART ONE:

We Long to Control
Our World

ONE

Understanding Personal Power

I've spent most of my life in a Fantasyland zipcode.

As a child I adored fairy tales like *The Ugly Duckling* and *Sleeping Beauty*. Growing up in a chaotic—sometimes dangerous—alcoholic family, I needed all the Prince-Charming-to-the-rescue fantasies and happy-ever-after endings I could get! So you probably won't be surprised to learn that my favorite radio program was called "Let's Pretend."

In a sense, "Let's Pretend" describes the *modus operandi* of everyone's childhood. Young children all have developmentally limited abilities to correctly interpret what's happening around them. They typically use the Let's-Pretend perspective of magical thinking (sometimes called infantile grandiosity) to explain life in general and people's responses to them in particular. With this immature perception of cause and effect, a young child concludes, "I am the center of my universe and I have the power to make things happen or not happen. *I am in control.*"

I believe the fantasy of unlimited human power to control is the most primitive and intensely cherished illusion of all people, children or adults. This belief convinces people that they *have the power to cause events and control people.*

Just because we can't remember back far enough to recall actually saying that to ourselves does not mean the magical thinking concept sprang from the overactive imagination of some child development specialist. We see evidence of magical thinking and control fantasies in young children every day.

DABNEY'S MAGICAL HAT

The world's most adorable granddaugher is named Dabney and just happens to be ours. (Talk about a coincidence!)

Before she learned to talk, Dabney used her "magical" hat to get outside. She had learned that before Mommy strolled her to the playground, Mommy put a hat on Dabney. So when Dabney wanted to go to the playground, she would find her hat, put it on, and stand by the door with her hand on the knob while making indistinct but urgent sounds. Often the hat performed its magic on Mommy, and out came the stroller.

Clearly, this dear little girl's perception of cause and effect was on a magical thinking level at that time. From such a developmentally limited viewpoint, *Dabney concluded that when she wore her wondrous hat, she could control Mommy!* Our granddaughter accurately observed a relationship between putting on her hat and going outside, didn't she? But she erroneously perceived that relationship as cause and effect.

Dabney's magical thinking and immature perceptions spun a fantasy of control. *They always do!* It was a fantasy because Dabney neglected to include her mother's intentionality in her conclusions about how to get outside.

Our granddaughter had not yet discovered the life-changing truth that *no* human being can completely control any situation that involves *another* human being. If you're not convinced, consider that even in the case of children and physically impaired or imprisoned adults, one can completely control their *bodies,* but not their *thoughts* and *emotions.*

My husband and I recently visited Dabney and her twin baby brothers. We noticed that her magical hat has been retired. When our granddaughter wants to go outside now, she says so with charming clarity. And Dabney has learned that playing outside depends on more than just *her* desire and efforts. Such details as schedules and weather seem to influence her *caregivers'* desires to take her outside.

Many such lessons, combined with normal cognitive development, will help Dabney outgrow both magical thinking and control fantasies. But it doesn't always seem to work that way, as I can testify.

Playing God is exhausting! I know because I do it far too often.

Of course when I do, I ignore the wisdom captured in a sign I've had for years.

DO NOT FEEL TOTALLY
PERSONALLY
IRREVOCABLY
RESPONSIBLE FOR EVERYTHING.
THAT'S MY JOB.

GOD

You've probably guessed that I don't do a very convincing imitation of God. But that doesn't stop me from frequently functioning like a "wanna-be" deity; as in, "I know I am not a divine being with supernatural powers, but I wanna-be."

Of course, if a close friend tried to tell me that I am often too controlling, I wouldn't believe her. And I probably would say something like this *to myself:*

> It's true that I know *other* people who are control freaks. In fact, *you* can be a little bossy occasionally. But *I* am just taking charge of my life and using my influence to help people!

To my friend, I might mumble something more like this: "Surely you don't expect me to be powerless and fatalistically resigned to circumstances or stand by as people destroy themselves, do you?"

DIFFERING USES OF PERSONAL POWER

Control? Influence? Indifferent resignation? How can we distinguish between them? We must understand the differences so that we will not assume an attitude of *resignation* or abdicate our *influence* as we work toward surrendering magical thinking and our crippling compulsions to *control.*

DIFFERING USES OF PERSONAL POWER

Situation: While hiking a mountain path, I come to an especially dangerous spot and notice, 100 feet below, the parched bones of a previous hiker who had lost his or her footing there.

Underuse of Personal Power **Resignation**	Realistic Use of Personal Power **Influence**	Overuse of Personal Power **Attempt to Control**
BASIC BELIEF I have no personal power to affect anybody or anything.	BASIC BELIEF I have substantial but limited power to control my life and to influence the lives of others.	BASIC BELIEF I have unlimited power to control my life and other people.
POSSIBLE BEHAVIORS 1. Believing I'm doomed to fall over the edge too, I crawl off the trail into a cave.	POSSIBLE BEHAVIORS 1. I slow my pace and procede very cautiously.	POSSIBLE BEHAVIORS 1. Believing I'm doomed to die, I leap over the edge to take control of my fate.
2. I sit and watch as a few hikers pass me and fall over the edge.	2. I find another, safer path and continue my hike.	2. Believing I can conquer any mountain trail on my own terms, I continue with no added concern.
	3. I post a sign warning others of the danger.	3. I insist upon carrying every child or adult who wants to hike that trail.
	4. I get other concerned hikers to help me build a guard rail at that spot.	4. Judging some hikers unfit to enter, I stop them (with force if necessary).
	5. Since I know the trail, I offer to guide hikers who want assistance.	

Figure 1-1

The chart on the opposite page represents a brief, basic class in Personal Power 101. I've used various responses to a hypothetical hiking experience to illustrate the differences between unrealistic and realistic uses of personal power and influence. By the way, I believe "realistic use of personal power" well defines the word *influence,* so I use those two concepts interchangeably throughout the book.

As you examine the chart, ask yourself which response style seems most familiar.

Where did you find yourself on our hypothetical mountain trail? Your location on the chart may offer a clue about your approach to many issues in your life. After all, isn't living a lot like walking a rugged and sometimes dangerous path? Each of the three response levels reflects a different way of thinking about our personal power to control other people and events. Of course many folks feel uneasy just *hearing* the phrase "personal power," let alone *thinking* about it.

Despite the discomfort some might experience with this topic, we need to recognize the realistic use of personal power known as influence. If we don't, we will be unable to identify the "under-powering" approach to life I am calling resignation. And unless we can distinguish appropriate use of influence from passive resignation, we will have a hard time avoiding the latter when we seek to change "overpowering" attitudes and attempts to control inappropriately.

INFLUENCE:
REALISTIC USE OF PERSONAL POWER

Even in the most unlikely situations, human beings have the capacity to display marvelously creative personal power to influence the outcome of their lives. I recently heard about a middle-aged woman who was abducted from a mall parking lot in broad daylight and locked in the trunk of her car. Her assailant then drove away in her car intending, as he later confessed, to kill her.

Although she had been physically overpowered, this spunky woman refused to assume the underpowered role in this terrifying drama. She was rescued after attracting attention to her car by removing her bra and managing to slip most of it through the tiny space between the car's body and its trunk lid. She said she hoped someone would notice a bra dangling from a car trunk. Actually, *several* some-ones did!

This woman could not completely control her life and death situation, could she? But she did not have to passively resign herself to the whims of her attacker. She chose to actively exercise her substantial but limited personal power to influence the outcome of that situation. No guarantees. But no resignation.

This example focuses on the motivating dynamic underlying all the control struggles we will examine—namely, staying safe. And this issue involves more than physical safety alone. We will resound this theme, with minor variations, again and again as we explore the personal, emotional, relational, and spiritual facets of our lives. As we do, we will discover that in the face of perceived threats to our safety, whether physical or nonphysical, paralyzing fear often destroys our sense of personal power. In effect, we surrender our capacity to influence the battle before the first shot is fired.

RESIGNATION: UNDERUSE OF PERSONAL POWER

During my years as a counselor, I've met many adults who describe themselves as "feeling powerless" regarding some extremely significant area of their lives. I also recall saying something like that to the counselor I saw during a debilitating bout of clinical depression some years ago. But we don't have to be depressed or in counseling to know that disturbing sensation of powerlessness.

When we describe ourselves as "feeling powerless," we often mean we've repeatedly tried and failed to control some significant situations in our lives—situations which nearly always involve controlling one or more "significant other." With typical all-or-nothing thinking, we often swing from one extreme to the other. If we can't *overpower* someone's will and control a situation, we'll *underpower* our way through those circumstances with an attitude of resignation.

In reality, all of us can exercise *some* measure of God-given personal power whatever our circumstances. Said differently, *adults always have choices.*

Clearly, some of us have more options in life than others. Innate endowments, such as intelligence, differ for each person. So do acquired characteristics—like education and financial status. Nevertheless, if we are mentally sound enough to write or read a book like this, we have choices. That is, as long as we *recognize* we have them.

SELECTIVE RESIGNATION:
GROWING DOWN

Curiously, we may actively and appropriately use our influence in *some* aspects of our lives, while abdicating it in *others*. This leaves us thinking, behaving, and feeling like responsible adults in many situations but like little kids at other times. In the latter situation, we selectively resign our influence and choices, and we *grow down*.

Growing down occurs as intelligent, well-functioning adults relinquish their abilities to reason and reach their own decisions when in the presence of certain authority figures. As if an invisible magician had waved his wand, a kind of *spontaneous childification* occurs. Rational thirty-five or fifty-year-olds suddenly become goofy third-graders. (Does any of this sound familiar?)

When speaking in conferences and seminary classes, I frequently describe the growing down phenomenon. Inevitably, listeners chuckle and exchange knowing glances because I'm painting a familiar picture of parts of their lives. *My* life too.

MY GROWING UP AND
GROWING DOWN

Growing up in alcoholic and other unhealthy families can be difficult and confusing. I know only too well.

I've never met or even seen a photo of my biological father. When he married my mom, he neglected to mention either his other wife or his past criminal activities. Only later did these facts help my mom understand why her new husband was so eager to move to Arizona from Massachusetts after they married.

When Mother got pregnant with me a year after they were married, my father's past caught up with him. So when I was born, my father was in a federal prison and my mother was thousands of miles from her family, facing the 1938 humiliation of a bogus marriage and an illegitimate child. These painful realities further reinforced my mother's already unhealthy self-concept.

When I was about two years old, Mother married my stepfather even though she'd known him only a very short time. She soon discovered he was an alcoholic. And that fact dramatically changed her life and mine. Incidentally, I was ten years old when my mother told me that the only dad I had ever known was not my real father.

My stepdad's alcoholism produced constant chaos and even occasionally life-threatening episodes in the family, which caused my mother great anxiety and unhappiness. Obviously, that kind of atmosphere was pretty scary for me too. But it was *doubly terrifying* when my mom, the only reasonably stable parent I had, was overwhelmed and depressed! I didn't understand why at the time, all I knew was that I felt safer and happier when my mother felt good enough to be more of a parent to me and my baby brother.

Obviously, somebody had to do something. My brother was too young, and I seemed to be the only person around who had the power to make my mom temporarily forget her miserable marriage and feel happy. So as a child, I lived every moment with this belief: "I am supposed to make my mother feel happy and good (or at least *better*) about herself and her life." Unfortunately, no one told me that it was impossible for one human being to control the emotional state of another. Influence, yes, but not control.

This was also unfortunate for my young son decades later when I grew down into that childhood fantasy once more. Here is how I described this episode in *Shame-Free Parenting*:[1]

> [This] occurred during a week I spent with my mother and her new husband in Arizona when our son, Dave, was about three and a half and our daughter, Becky, was a year old. We were living in Seattle during those years, so the visit entailed all the stress of flying with small children and setting up the child-care routine in a strange home.
>
> Dave was thrilled to ride his grandparents' pony. However, he was *not* so thrilled with all of his new surroundings and schedule — and he made that crystal-clear. I grew increasingly anxious when he exhibited, with annoying regularity, that he was *not* a perfect child. I thought I was being appropriately firm, even though I did tolerate more fussiness than when we were at home. But, clearly, that did not make the correct statement about my mother. (Note: not about Dave or about me. About *my mother*.)
>
> Two days into the visit, she delivered a subtle reminder which reactivated my childhood guidance system. Mother took me aside and said, "I read somewhere that you never *really* know what kind of a parent you are until you have grandchildren. When

I see you and Dave, well — it makes me wonder."

Of course! How could I have missed it? I wasn't making my mother feel good about herself and her mothering when I allowed my child to behave like the overstimulated, confused three-year-old he was. . . .

It never occurred to me to do anything other than immediately clamp-down on my three year old as if he had just appeared on the FBI's "Most Wanted" list. Oh, he became more subdued and docile, all right. (Now I realize that was probably due to a combination of shock and terror.) I scrutinized Dave's every waking moment for telltale signs of imperfection. And I did such a thorough job that by the end of the week, I had earned my mother's "seal of approval" for noteworthy child-improvement.

Am I saying my mother was a monster? Absolutely not. My mom deeply loved me and my children. Yet, she was also a very insecure and shame-bound woman who looked to her children, and later her grandchildren, to mend her tattered self-concept.

Didn't I love my children? Of course I did. But when my mother said the magic words that, as I put it — "reactivated my childhood guidance system," *I grew down*. And when that happened, I once again functioned from the magically grandiose belief that I had the power and the responsibility to make my mother feel happy and good about herself. At that moment, I transferred my primary concern and investment of energy from being the parent of my child to being the child of my parent. (I still feel like crying when I think of that.)

Can you see that I abdicated my personal power and relinquished my adult capacity to reason through that situation and reach my own parenting conclusions? Instead, I simply accepted my mother's interpretation of reality just as I had *had* to do when I was a child with no other choice. But I was *not* a child, so my reaction did not match reality.

GROWING UP TO REALITY

Believing we have no valid perceptions, choices, or capacities to influence people and change circumstances is as unrealistic as thinking we have unlimited power to completely control them. That day when I surrendered my own perception of reality and "childified" myself, it was as if *I reached into my skull, removed my brain, and handed it to my mother!* Actually, as an adult, I had perceptual abilities, choices, and resources I did not have as a child. But I did not recognize that reality. That's the point.

When we attempt to control others we, in effect, ask them to entrust their brains to us. That ridiculously unrealistic attitude will claim most of our attention in the following chapters. Throughout our learning and changing adventures ahead, we must remember the truth that will bring balance along the way. The solution to magical thinking and illusions of control does not include abdicating our God-given responsibility to reason, choose, and exercise influence.

We are not all-powerful demigods.

We are not powerless children.

We are adult human beings with astounding but limited power to change our lives and our world. That is reality. And as we allow the Holy Spirit of God to guide, empower, and work through us, we will learn that is enough.

Think about It

Look again at Figure 1-1 on page 18, focusing particularly on the basic beliefs undergirding each response style.

Think about one or more troubling situations in your life at the moment. By your emotions and actions in response to those situations, do you see evidence of the basic beliefs behind underuse or overuse of personal power?

Now, with the same situations in mind, read aloud the basic belief in the "Influence" column. How does that change your perspective on those situations?

Write down at least one way you would approach these situations differently if you consistently operated by the basic belief associated with the realistic use of personal power.

Pray about It

DEAR LORD, I'm not sure I know how to use the influence You have given me without overpowering others or underpowering myself. Please help me learn how to live responsibly. AMEN.

Learn More about It

Before we can think seriously about relinquishing magical thinking's control fantasies and moving toward more realistic uses of our personal power, we need to understand more about it. In chapter 2, we'll explore the factors that contribute to prolonged magical thinking.

T W O

Prolonged Magical Thinking
and Illusions of Control

We may outgrow mumps, measles, and zits, but we don't *automatically* outgrow all of our magical thinking and its control fantasies.

Those immature perceptions of our personal power should expire as we grow older, but in many cases, they seem to have more lives than 100 cats. What gives these fantasies their die-hard staying power? That's the mystery we'll investigate in this chapter.

Reinforcers of childhood control fantasies seem to come in two types. First, there are those we all encounter about equally just by living in our contemporary culture. The second category of reinforcers seems to vary according to our individual childhood experiences.

#1 UNIVERSAL REINFORCER
OF MAGICAL-THINKING:
OUR OWN I-DOLATRY[1]

I believe that the third chapter of Genesis illuminates the murky origins of the human control fantasy. There we learn that the Tempter, Satan, promised Eve she would become "like God" if she ate fruit from the only off-limits tree in God's garden. And that turned out to be an offer she and Adam couldn't refuse.

Of course we can't know with certainty what divine characteristics Eve had in mind when she heard the phrase, "like God." But as I read Scripture, I find that God is identified by His omnipotence—His *unlimited power,* more than by any other attribute. So perhaps the primitive fantasy of unlimited power to control traces its roots to the bedrock of original sin when our Edenic ancestors longed to be like God.

While this may be true, it is also true that each of us, in our own turn, reenacts that Genesis scene as we wrestle throughout our lives with the primal lust for unlimited power to control our worlds and their inhabitants. And as we wrestle, we will find no shortage of cheerleaders on the sidelines telling us we can, indeed, be like God. All we need is a little enlightenment.

#2 UNIVERSAL REINFORCER OF MAGICAL-THINKING: NEW AGE SPIRITUALITY

Want to waken your dozing divinity? The wildly popular *A Course in Miracles* represents just one of countless options that promises to do just that. And one of the latest ripples in the New Age pond focuses on the so-called Goddess movement, the offspring of pairing the I-can-be-like-God message with a bizarre brand of feminism. Here's how one of this movement's leaders described it: "With the goddess movement, everybody gets to do what they want. . . . We're all the goddess."[2]

If we listen closely, I think we'll hear the Eden-lie echoing down the corridors of time and right out the door of goddess worship and all the other movements lumped together as New Age spirituality. Its "human-beings-have-the-potential-for-unlimited-power" message is simply the original tempter's original lie dressed up in the gobbeldygook of a New Age guru or goddess. This message promises that we can do whatever we want while it panders to our lust for God's omnipotence. No wonder the New Age movement is so popular!

I believe we all have the same sin-bent longing to be crowned Master of the Universe, or at least of our *own* universe. And I think that all of us routinely hear variations on the New Age theme of unlimited human potential to be like God. If those two reinforcers exhausted the list, we could expect to find everyone facing equal amounts of magical thinking. However, there are at least two other reinforcers of our childhood fantasies that are not as evenly distributed. They seem to vary based on the degree of healthy functioning in our birth families.

I am not one of those family therapists who thinks every family is dysfunctional. I rejoice with great joy when I see consistently adequate parents providing the safe, secure, and stable families their children need and God desires. True, there are no perfect parents — no, not one — so there are no perfect families. Yet we all recognize that some families are much healthier than others.

I've long believed that parents do a far better job when they aim for "consistently adequate," rather than trying to hit the illusory bullseye of perfection. Parents who consistently handle personal struggles, family issues, and child-raising challenges adequately and appropriately qualify as healthy and well-functioning in my opinion.

PARENTAL TRAITS THAT HELP TO APPROPRIATELY RESOLVE MAGICAL THINKING

Imperfect but consistently adequate parents in imperfect but basically healthy families share many common characteristics. Let's look at five parental traits that significantly affect the appropriate resolution of childrens' magical thinking and illusions of control.

1. Well-functioning parents know that neither they nor their families are problem-free and perfect, so they don't pretend they are.

I cannot overemphasize the significance of this parental attitude. We will see again and again what a difference this biblically based and realistic view of human beings and families makes in our lives. In fact, unless parents possess trait number one, they will be unable to sustain any of the other four characteristics of well-functioning families. And without these qualities, parents — and the families they head — will inevitably reinforce prolonged magical thinking and control fantasies.

2. Well-functioning parents understand their children and the basics of child development so they have realistic expectations.

Each child is uniquely precious. No child is a short adult. This means that to be consistently adequate, parents need to know as much as possible about each of their children's unique qualities. And parents need to understand enough about appropriate developmental expectations so that when they say "act your age," they really know what that means.

For instance, it's normal for preschoolers to spill their milk on a fairly regular basis. Rather than lectures or spankings, those little milk-spillers need paper towels so they can learn to clean up after themselves. Even the brightest four year old cannot have the coordination of an adolescent.

3. Well-functioning parents are consistently adequate because they seek help when personal problems persist.

What's the prerequisite for getting help with a problem? Admitting I have one, of course.

Whether it's alcoholism, "rage-aholism," or depression, unless a parent "owns" the problem, he or she will never reach out for help to solve these or other persistent and potentially life-dominating problems. And these — plus a host of other personal struggles — will *seriously impair anyone's ability to parent.* Because, if I don't acknowledge and get help for a recurring personal problem, I will spend more and more time and energy hiding or disguising it. That means I will have less time and energy to invest in my children's lives and my family's well-being. And that means problems.

4. Well-functioning parents focus on problem solving when inevitable family problems arise.

Parents usually approach *family* problems in the same way they handle *personal* problems. And as we all know so well, there *will* be family problems! Healthy families do not function well because they have no problems. They function well because when the inevitable problems of living arise, the parents leading these families focus on *problem solving.* (That's the kind of thing my husband calls a "no-brainer!") Parents will do that when they hold a realistic view of people and families (trait number one).

In contrast, unhealthy families handle problems by investing their energies in *appearance management* which involves, shall we say, a creative rearranging of reality. The difference in those approaches reflects a parent's commitment to truth.

5. Well-functioning parents are committed to knowing and telling the truth.

All young children believe their parents know everything about everything and always tell the truth. And children always assume that their family is the way *all* families are. And are *supposed* to be. Said differently, parents create reality and establish universal truth as they define and explain life to their children. And in healthy families, that works out fine because parents have a deep commitment to truth. Wise parents recognize that you don't explain things to a toddler the same way you do to a teen. So in healthy families, parents understand enough about child development to know how to communicate in an age-appropriate manner.

THE ROLE OF DENIAL IN UNHEALTHY FAMILIES

In unhealthy families, where the emphasis is on appearing problem-free, truth is an enemy—not a friend. Parents in these families want to hide obvious problems for as long as possible. Hiding, a.k.a. denial, involves literally limitless possible alterations of reality all designed to make some unacceptable truth disappear. (Unacceptable because poorly-functioning parents believe the lie that they and their families should be perfect and problem-free.) This process bears a striking similarity to a magic trick with disappearing rabbits.

Hiding/denying might sound like this: "You think you heard me fall down when I came up the porch steps last night? I didn't fall down. You must be imagining things again."

Denial maneuvers eventually spring a reality-leak for two inescapable reasons. One: problems tend to grow. Two: so do children. This means that parents almost always have to admit a problem exists as it becomes progressively more obvious and children notice more. But if parents believe they are supposed to be problem-free and perfect, they respond by distorting reality to disguise the problem and deflect responsibility. "Drunk? You think I was drunk? I didn't fall down the porch steps because I was drunk! Those rotten steps were slippery again."

Can you see that in well-functioning families, where parents have a solid commitment to living by truth, children will grow up grounded in reality? In unhealthy families, however, children grow up in an atmosphere polluted with deception and distortions of reality intended to create the illusion of problem-free perfection. Creating illusions captures the essence of magic and, as we've learned, of children's magical thinking. So we can understand how an early diet of deception and illusion feeds prolonged magical thinking, which leads us to a closer look at the remaining two reinforcers of our control illusions.

#1 CHILDHOOD REINFORCER OF MAGICAL-THINKING: PARENTAL DISTORTIONS OF REALITY

You don't have to grow-up in an alcoholic family to know "up close and personal" about parental distortions of reality. As we explore this first childhood reinforcer of magical thinking, we need to remember that distortions of reality come in varying degrees of severity.

Mild to Moderate Distortions of Reality

Even in apparently well-functioning families, loving parents can unintentionally reinforce magical thinking with statements such as, "Your dad/mom and I would be so pleased and proud of you if you got straight *A*s/set a new school record/win the Scripture memorization contest. We know you can do it if you just try harder next time."

It's somewhat subdued, but can you hear the heartbeat of magical thinking? It pounds: *I must control better so I can make it come out differently next time.* And the "it" we work to "make come out differently next time" almost always involves the will and skill of another person.

When our children were swimming competitively, my husband and I encouraged them to do their best. But we never told them they had to be *the* best, i.e., win or we would be displeased. Let's face it, no matter how hard Becky and Dave tried, they could not completely control the outcome of their races. Sometimes other swimmers were stronger, more talented, and better trained in their events. You can imagine how gratified we were to hear interviews in which Dave, a silver and gold medalist in the 1984 Olympics, thanked us for supporting and encouraging him without pressuring him to win.

Sadly, many of us still think that maybe if *we* could have won

Olympic medals or accomplished other outstanding feats, we could have fully pleased our parents. But even when children work really, *really* hard and actually manage to make it (whatever result we seek to control) come out different the next time, there's no guarantee that their folks would be pleased and really love them.

Consider the fact that *children cannot earn their parents' love.* It's a gift. What's more, *children do not have the power, in and of themselves, to please their parents, because "being pleased" is a function of someone's personal value system.* Of course we lacked the reasoning ability to grasp this reality as children. We naturally assumed that when we weren't smart enough/athletic enough/pretty or slim enough/religious enough/*whatever* enough to please our parents, that was a statement about our disgusting inadequacies. In reality, it was a statement about our parents' values.

I believe that we all naturally, intensely long for our parents' love and approval because God created that longing ultimately to draw us to Himself and to godly living. Ideally, parental love remains constant since it reflects parents' tender, cherishing attitude toward their children — apart from anything they do. In other words, *healthy parents love their kids for no good reason!* Simply for being who they are. Unlike love, approval fluxuates based on parents' value-based assessments of their children's behavior.

Unfortunately, in many families, love and approval get all tangled and confused. Some of us were raised in homes where what we did became a statement about who we are. For instance, instead of being handed a paper towel when we spilled milk, we were called clumsy — or much worse. Or perhaps, our parents withdrew emotionally when our behavior failed to measure up to their standards. And even when these standards were colossally unrealistic, we could not have known that as children. Because, believing grownups know everything and always tell the truth, we naturally assumed our parents would not expect something of us unless we could do it.

Unable to understand that love is a gift and approval is in the value system of the beholder, children will keep jumping through dimly lit, moving hoops trying to figure out how to be and do *something* enough — to earn Mommy and Daddy's clearly expressed affection. This means that when even well-meaning parents substitute performance-related approval for unconditional love, they distort reality and inadvertently fuel their children's magical thinking.

Yet this pales in comparison to distortions of reality in more seriously unhealthy families.

Severe Distortions of Reality

Hang a heavy stone around someone's neck and then drown that person in deep water. That sounds like something out of a Mafia hitman's handbook, doesn't it? Actually, Jesus said doing this would be better than placing literal or figurative obstacles in the paths of "little ones" thus causing them to stumble. (See Matthew 18:4-7.) And while Jesus probably referred to spiritual stumbling, little children can be "caused to stumble" in all aspects of their lives. The common stumbling block? The severe distortions of reality known as lies.

Recently, I saw a deeply moving documentary that followed several children living directly in the path of the nuclear cloud from the Chernobyl nuclear power plant disaster. The narrator explained that, in comparison to adults, children have immature immune systems that make them much more susceptible to the effects of toxic fallout. Similarly, children's limited cognitive development prevents them from filtering out the toxic verbal and non-verbal distortions of reality that drift downwind from poorly-functioning parents in unhealthy families.

For example, if I attempt to blame you for "causing" me to hit you, you would probably conclude that I was pretty immature to try to get you to take what belongs to me: namely, personal responsibility for my choices. And you would be right. However if, as children, we were blamed for Mom's rages, Dad's alcoholism, or maybe even for our *own* hands-on (sexual or physical) abuse, we did not have the same choice to disbelieve and disregard such blatant attempts to shift an adult's responsibility to a child.

How does this child-blaming sound? Here are a few examples along with the conclusions children likely reach in light of their magical-thinking perspectives.

ADULT'S WORDS: "Of course Daddy left, you crybaby, you drove him away with your whining."

CHILD'S CONCLUSIONS: (1) I caused my parents' divorce. (2) When I cry or want something, people I love a lot will leave me.

ADULT'S WORDS: "You enjoy making me beat you, don't you?"

CHILD'S CONCLUSIONS: (1) I cause my mom/dad to hurt me. (2) Who I am makes it OK to hurt me.

ADULT'S WORDS: "If you'd help your mother more with the housework, she wouldn't have so many migraines."

CHILD'S CONCLUSIONS: (1) I control whether or not my mom has headaches. (2) If I help people enough, I can prevent them from experiencing pain.

ADULT'S WORDS: "If you tell your mom or anyone else about our special secret, the police will take me away and then the family won't have any money."

CHILD'S CONCLUSIONS: (1) I am responsible for my abuser's safety and my family's existence. (2) It's better for people when I get sexually abused.

Those are just a few of the endless examples of how severe distortions of reality can damage children's beliefs about themselves, others, and the world. And when we grow up in families where under-responsible, blame-shifting adults run the show, we inevitably encounter another fantasy reinforcer.

#2 CHILDHOOD REINFORCER OF MAGICAL THINKING: NEED FOR SELF-PROTECTION

Did you hear the true story about the six-year-old boy who lives in an extremely violent neighborhood where gunshots routinely punctuate the rhythm of his daily life? One evening as the boy's mother was putting him to bed, she noticed an empty deodorant bottle on the table. When she asked him to explain, he replied, "the label says it's guaranteed to keep me 100 percent safe."

That dear little kid really understands the basics, doesn't he? Staying safe. His life-affirming focus on personal safety marks him as a healthy human being. After all, our Creator God gave us life, and the cell-deep desire to stay alive reflects good stewardship of that gift.

Most parents work hard to provide safe and loving homes for their children. Tragically, too many homes lack not just love, but even consistent safety for arms, legs, genitals, ideas, and dreams. If we grew up in one of these unsafe families, to one degree or another, we *needed* the fantasies spun by our magical thinking. No matter how ridiculous our magical, childish perceptions may seem to adult minds, they rescued us from drowning in the bottomless horror of utter helplessness.

Sometimes these immature and grandiose conclusions lead children to blame their mistreatment on qualities about themselves as basic as gender. Recent research with sexually abused girls, ranging in age from six- to twelve-years old, found their self-concepts were much different than non-abused girls. The young sexual abuse survivors stated they did not like being female and expressed interest in being more like boys. They also exhibited much more masculine behavior than non-abused girls. The researchers concluded that sexual abuse from male perpetrators led the girls to associate their gender with vulnerability and victimization.[3]

As we can see, such immature reasoning includes an element of "fairy-tale logic," to explain why some people are treated so differently than others. Of course, all loyal fans of fairy tales know the explanation: *good things happen to good people and bad things happen to bad people.* The young girls in the research study seem to have concluded that being female is bad — bad enough, in fact, to cause sexual abuse. From their magical fairy-tale perspective, being more masculine would give them control over their sexual safety. No wonder they wanted to be more like boys!

Again, kids in well-functioning families outgrow this fairy-tale logic mindset as their thinking matures. But magical thinking and fairy-tale logic marry, set up housekeeping, and birth prolific lies in our belief systems, if, as children, we are blamed for our own mistreatment and our parents' problems.

True, it's incredibly painful to believe that our gender or something else about our very being is so rotten and worthless we cause our parents or others to neglect or abuse us. But there is something far worse for a little child. It is the desolate terror of acknowledging that *those adults we loved and trusted made their own hurtful choices about how to treat us, and we were completely powerless to stop them.*

Think about how fragile you were as a little child. Can you imagine how overwhelmingly terrifying it would have been to face and feel your utter defenselessness? No wonder children need to believe magical thinking's protective control fantasy that, "If I caused it (hands-on or hands-off abuse), then I can control whether or not it happens."

Few of us easily acknowledge that we believe this good-to-good/bad-to-bad and I-control-the-world stuff. We likely profess to live by far more mature and biblical tenets. But mark it down: we *may not always live what we profess, but we will always live what we believe.*

> Although unaware of it, many of us learned to believe a lie that prolongs magical thinking and guarantees a life of fairy-tale fantasies. That lie says: *I can be good enough to stay safe and get loved.*

So what's the problem with magical thinking's control fantasies? They don't keep us any safer than the little boy's empty deodorant container that guaranteed 100 percent protection. And I believe that unrecognized magical fantasies inevitably leave us wounded, weary, and wondering what's wrong with us and with God.

MARYANNE'S STORY: THE PAINFUL DISAPPOINTMENT OF MAGICAL THINKING

Magical thinking sounds like something we do while watching a *Snow White* video, doesn't it? But as we're learning, when we try to structure our lives based on magical thinking, we set ourselves up for major disappointments—some of which can be very painful. Just ask Maryanne. (I have changed all names and personal details to protect individuals whose experiences I share throughout this book.)

"I really don't want to be here," were the less-than-enthusiastic words Maryanne spoke as she entered the counseling office for the first time. When I inquired what brought her to the office under those circumstances, her large brown eyes brimmed with tears as she put her hands up to her shoulders. "These do," she replied softly. Maryanne's family physician had suggested she seek counseling as a means of reducing the emotional stress that seemed to exacerbate the chronic pain in her shoulder and upper back muscles.

"I ought to be able to control my feelings better than this. I'm so embarrassed and ashamed to have to come here. And I wouldn't if the pain weren't so unbearable. The physical therapy and exercises didn't seem to help very much, and my doctor doesn't want me to get dependent on muscle-relaxing drugs. Neither do I, of course. So here I am."

I learned that Maryanne grew up with an absentee "traveling executive" father and a perfectionistic, hypochondriac mother who used her only daughter as a combination cook, housekeeper, and nanny. While her two younger brothers could play after school and during vacations, Maryanne was expected to "help Mother." As Maryanne described more of her family's dynamics, it became clear that, in reality, "help Mother" was a code phrase. It actually meant: run the home, keep peace between your brothers, and do it all so perfectly that Mother will feel rested and well enough to be an appealing wife to Father so he'll keep coming back home on the weekends.

By the time Maryanne was in elementary school, she knew her parents' marriage was in trouble. So she worked harder than ever to make the family run smoothly and to control the quality of her folks' deteriorating relationship to keep the family safe. She explained,

> I used to lie in bed and listen to my mother scream accusations of adultery at my dad. Eventually, he didn't even bother to deny it. He'd yell back, "Well, if you were a real wife to me when I came home I wouldn't need to look around to have some fun." As I heard that over and over I knew it was my fault that my mom was too tired to go out and "have fun" with my dad when he came home. I didn't really understand much about sex back then. Now I think that my mom had sexual problems of some kind. Then, all I knew was that somehow I had to clean even more carefully and do a better job of taking care of my brothers. That way my mother wouldn't go into her "Friday frenzy," as I called it. You see, my dad came home every Friday night after being gone all week. And my mom spent every Friday running around the house vacuuming and scrubbing even though I already worked as hard as a little kid could to keep the house neat and clean. Of course, she'd always find a little dust somewhere that I had missed or one of my brothers' toys I hadn't picked up. Then she'd say something like, "You just don't care do you? You don't care at all that I have back problems and shouldn't be working so hard to make this pigsty presentable when your father comes home. If you really cared about this

family, you'd help a little." By Friday evening, she was flat in bed, full of pain pills. And she usually stayed that way all weekend. That's when my dad would tell me to "help your mother more." No matter how much I tried to explain or how much more I did around the house than any other kid I knew, my dad just kept repeating: "You could do more if you really tried." I think those words became my personal motto. And the more things fell apart in the family, the more tense and tired I got from "really trying" to do more.

As we worked together in counseling, Maryanne began to realize how her parents used her as a scapegoat rather than admit and get help for their marital problems. She also saw how she had developed the habit of pushing herself past the point of exhaustion by tuning out her body's cues for rest. By the time she married and had two sons, Maryanne lived in a state of constant stress because she never seemed to be able to do everything she thought she ought to do. She believed that no matter how much she did—in the house, as a roommother and teacher's aide for her boys, or as the bookkeeper for her husband's small company—it was never enough. And when there were problems at school, in the marriage, or in the business, Maryanne "just knew" the solution was for her to do even more.

After decades of chronic stress while allowing herself only four or five hours of sleep a night, Maryanne's body began to break down. About the same time, her husband's company nearly went bankrupt, which greatly increased the tension in the home. Of course, Maryanne still believed that she could do more if she really tried and that doing more would magically control the family's fate. However, by that time her body was no longer obeying the self-destructive commands she gave it.

In time, Maryanne began to tell herself the truth about the childhood messages she received from her parents. And she saw how they had reinforced and prolonged her magical thinking. It was difficult for Maryanne to let herself off the hook for not being able to do enough to control her childhood family. But she struggled far more with facing the need to relinquish her illusion about controlling the family she had now. As she continued the hard work of changing, Maryanne began to see how unhealthy her marriage had become. Although reluctant at first, her husband Jeff, eventually acknowledged the need for marriage counseling. Here's how Maryanne described the changes in her life.

> I can't believe how different I feel from my first time here. Oh, I don't mean everything is perfect by any means. Jeff and I still have a lot to work on in our relationship, but we both feel hopeful since we've already seen some good changes. One of the biggest changes is my learning to trust him enough to quit the bookkeeping work I hated. I was always afraid that if I didn't watch the business like a hawk, he'd ruin it. Now I have more time to go for walks and do the stretching exercises that really help me relax. The boys have even noticed the difference. They tell me I smile more lately. It's so strange, my whole life I thought that if I worked hard enough, I could make everyone and everything around me happy and safe. And I nearly killed myself and my marriage trying. Now, I feel like I'm doing so much less but I feel so much safer. And my family actually seems to be happier too. I can't control the economy, so there's no guarantee about our business. But I'm learning to trust God for the future and for a whole lot of other things too. And, I know this is hard to believe, but I am treating myself to a massage every now and then even though I no longer need physical therapy.

You may never need physical therapy as a result of your magical thinking. Yet, like Maryanne, all of us need to recognize the way childish magical thinking and adult-size control illusions damage our relationships and our lives.

Think about It

Complete this sentence for a clue about what your parents highly valued when you were a child: If I can be _____ enough I will keep people I value in my life and make them love (or respect or obey) me.

Has this prolonged magical-thinking style of living brought you personal, relational, and spiritual well-being? If not, are you ready to consider surrendering it for something more realistic? If not, why not?

Pray about It

DEAR LORD, You know how confused and scared I get sometimes, especially when I'm facing something new in my life that challenges familiar ideas and ways of thinking. Please help me stay open to learning the truth You want me to discover about myself and about You. AMEN.

Learn More about It

When prolonged magical thinking establishes a stronghold in our minds, we become skillful illusionists. So skillful that most of the time we don't even recognize our own skill. Let's take a closer look at illusions and illusionists next.

THREE

Recognizing Illusions and Illusionists

Illusions. Magic is all about creating illusions.

And so is magical thinking, as we've seen. However, most of us who live with the damaging effects of prolonged magical thinking neither recognize nor admit that we regularly traffic in illusions.

In contrast, honest "magicians" always tell their audiences that they are illusionists. These professional illusionists, however, rarely describe the years spent rigorously rehearsing their performances to perfect the manipulations of perception that earn startled gasps and enthusiastic applause.

I've been one of those gaspers and applauders from time to time. But I have to admit magic isn't what it used to be for me since I've been reading books written to expose phony spiritualists, so-called psychics, and "pseudo-occult phenomena."[1]

I've learned about "The Magician's Choice" and other mind-reading techniques that create illusions to support mentalists' claims of extrasensory powers. And like me, you've probably seen at least one television exposé about some slick magician or phony "faith healer," who plants one or more confederates in the audience to fabricate the supernatural. Professional illusionists as well as spiritualist charlatans and cult leaders use all these techniques and many more for one ultimate purpose: to create illusions.

ILLUSIONS

Illusions, of course, fabricate the appearance of something that does not exist or proclaim the absence of something that does exist. Successful illusions significantly alter our perceptions of reality, in effect, constructing an illusionist-designed *un*reality.

I recently read about a turn-of-the-century pamphlet describing how to create the illusion of sword-swallowing.

> Make an imitation sword out of licorice covered with tinfoil or aluminum paint; the licorice sword is swallowed and the real one produced from behind the back, giving the impression the sword has passed entirely through you.[2]

Illusionists have come a long way since the days of foil-covered licorice swords. David Copperfield, perhaps the most famous contemporary illusionist, walks through the Great Wall of China and makes airplanes and The Statue of Liberty "disappear." On national television! And Copperfield isn't about to disclose the secrets of his illusions. He even refuses to reveal the location of the enormous warehouse containing his millions of dollars of sophisticated equipment.[3]

Clearly, illusions have become high-tech! Illusions have become high-priced too. Multi-millionaire Copperfield is described as one of today's highest paid entertainers. In truth, all illusions have significant pay-offs. They provide the creators with a degree of control over the consumers.

Whether we realize it or not, all of us both create and consume illusions virtually every day, because the vast majority of illusions occur outside the circles of professional magicians. These distortions of reality are the usually undeclared, often unintentional and routinely unrecognized illusions of our daily lives in contrast to the openly acknowledged illusions of the on-stage performer.

To more readily recognize everyday, off-stage illusions, we need to take a closer look at the differences we discover between those reality manipulations that are declared and intentional and those that are not. And even the effects of *these* manipulations differ, depending on whether or not we recognize the illusion as such.

"SIFTING" ILLUSIONISTS

Each of us functions as an illusionist when we seek to alter perceptions of reality—our own and those of others. *And most of us never realize we're doing it.* This unwelcomed fact makes learning to identify illusionists an important part of maturing and living in truth rather than deception.

The following "Illusionist Identification Grid" helps us to, in effect, "sift" and separate four major types of illusion creators. As you can see, I used the presence or absence of intentionality and openness as the cross-wires in this grid. Take a moment right now to study each type of illusionist, the overwhelming majority of whom never think of themselves—I should say *our*selves—as illusionists.

The Illusionist Identification Grid

OPENNESS

		Yes	No
I N T E N T I O N	Y E S	HONEST ILLUSIONISTS are aware of intentions to create illusions and openly declare their intentions.	DELIBERATE DECEIVERS are aware of intentions to create illusions but do not openly declare their intentions.
	N O	TRUTH-ANCHORED PEOPLE do not intend to create illusions but acknowledge to themselves and others that they are prone to do so.	MOST PEOPLE do not intend to create illusions and do not believe that they do, so neither privately consider nor openly declare the possibility.

Figure 3-1

HONEST ILLUSIONISTS

As we've learned, honest illusionists identify themselves as just that, even when the rest of us insist upon calling them magicians. In the language of our grid, honest illusionists are in the Yes-Yes box because they are *open* about their *intention* to manipulate perceptions of reality. In comparison to the numbers in the other three categories, the population in the honest illusionists' box is extremely sparse.

DELIBERATE DECEIVERS

Whereas honest illusionists openly declare their intentions to manipulate onlookers' perceptions, deliberate deceivers keep it a secret. Over the centuries we've recognized many of these deceivers, but usually only after their destructive charades produced profound suffering. For example, most statesmen initially believed Adolph Hitler when he promised not to devour Europe if he could swallow just a few territorial tidbits.

By far the greatest number of malicious deceivers have always operated in much smaller spheres of influence than Hitler's, in circles about the size of a family or a church. We call them unfaithful spouses, abusive parents, or heretics — among other things. This illusionist-sifting business really gets complicated when we consider that many, if not most, of the folks you or I might call abusive or heretical do not see themselves that way. This brings us to the most densely populated category of all: MOST PEOPLE.

MOST PEOPLE

Most of us regular folks do not openly call ourselves illusion creators because we don't know we are. Besides, our illusions are generally no more dangerous to swallow than a licorice sword. For example, I usually swallow the "one size fits all" and "easy to assemble" illusions. How about you? The emotional indigestion I experience after discovering how those phrases altered reality annoys more than pains me.

Over the past few years as some extra inches have crept around my middle, I've specialized in weight-loss related illusions. Oh, I haven't fallen for the obvious ones. For instance, I refuse to believe that breaking cookies before eating them allows caloric leakage. And I'm doubtful that drinking diet soda with dessert actually cancels the calories. However, I've noticed that I buy lots of "light-living" and fat-free type cookbooks, yet seldom actually prepare any of the meals.

Yes, I *know* it doesn't make sense! Said differently, it does not match the reality of weight reduction. That's why reading low-fat recipes with the hope of losing weight qualifies as an illusion. But *eating* low-fat meals as one important part of losing weight does not. And that remains true no matter how sincerely I wish it were otherwise.

SINCERE ILLUSIONISTS

Not long ago, about 1,000 sincere illusionists gathered in Scottsdale, Arizona. Their illusions weren't about merely *slimmer* bodies. They sought "cellular awakening" and *immortal* bodies. At their "convergence" the movement's founders urged attenders to ignore "death programming" and get out of society's "death cult" because "death is unnatural."[4]

Noticing a wig on one of the male founders, the article's author observed that apparently hair follicles do not become immortal! However, such immortality gaps don't seem to bother the devoted followers who have moved from all over the world to live permanently near the movement's three founders. (They're hoping it's *really, really permanently!*)

We can rightly question the sincerity of those three leaders since they live off the gifts of their followers. No doubt some attending the "immortality convergence" came more out of curiosity than conviction. But I don't for a minute doubt the sincerity of adults who uproot their lives to follow their leaders. Do you?

Those sincere immortality seekers remind me of the lad we met in chapter 2 who kept the empty deodorant bottle beside his bed to guarantee 100 percent protection. They intend to do whatever is necessary to control their lifespans. Which is another way of saying they want to be like God.

As much as we loathe admitting it, we must face the inescapable conclusion that human beings do not have the limitless power to completely control either other human beings, natural events, or our own longevity. *We influence people and events—God controls them.* If you're like me, you may often have difficulty keeping that vital distinction straight. And as we're learning, that confusion fuels our compulsions to control.

THE CONSUMING COMPULSION TO CONTROL

I believe that prolonged magical thinking and illusions of unlimited human power pervade many of our adult lives, some of our churches, and much of the culture with a *consuming compulsion to control* just about everything and everybody. And this control compulsion can *really* consume! Time, energy, resources, relationships. Lives. It will consume them all if we let it. Just ask some of the immortality seekers in Scottsdale.

Obviously, we see this in varying degrees in different people, churches, and segments of our culture. Obviously too, since the power to control is largely a fantasy, the more we are compelled to control, the more time we will spend in "The Twilight Zone" of unreality. And life can get every bit as weird in that delusional zipcode as it ever got on the popular television program by that name. The immortality convergence proved that!

Sometimes it can get pretty dangerous too.

SCIENCE AND THE
PROMISE OF CONTROL AND SAFETY

Most control-driven, sincere illusionists appear far more rational than those Scottsdale immortalists. Some sound very scientific.

Students in most of the Western world are taught to look to the scientific method as an instrument to understand, predict, and control virtually all aspects of nature to make life safer, healthier, and more pleasant. And at least in the United States, we seem to have learned this lesson well. According to a 1994 Louis Harris poll, sixty-eight percent of the American adults who participated said they believed that, "Science will solve many of the world's problems."[5]

In truth, we could make a case for the fact that science has replaced God as the primary source of comfort and object of hope for many adults. This is especially true of medical science. However, science does not have all the answers about controlling our lives and world. And many of the answers it has turn out to be wrong. Consider Thalidomide, DDT, lead in gasoline and paint, and scores of other "solutions" to various problems that in their time were scientifically correct. Evidently, even the so-called "hard sciences" are a lot squishier than we were led to believe in Chemistry or Biology 101.

And medical science currectly faces "a disaster in the making," according to a 1994 *Newsweek* magazine article describing virulent and highly drug-resistant new forms of bacteria that "killed 19,000 U.S. hospital patients and contributed to the deaths of 58,000 more in 1992."[6] A spokesman for the U.S. Center for Disease Control and Prevention made a telling comment in light of our current discussion. He said, "Many of the diseases *we thought we had under control* are coming back." (Emphasis added.) And a few of them are coming back in forms that teeter perilously close to being out-of-control.

How did such deadly drug-resistant bacteria develop? The medical scientists studying the phenomenon now attribute this potentially catastrophic health care problem to previous misuse of a highly-lauded health care solution — antibiotics. Commenting on this medical crisis, *Newsweek* quotes a physican who said, "Medicine is especially susceptible to *modern science's fantasy of controlling nature.*"[7] (Emphasis added.)

Clearly, sincere and uncritical trust in science as the controlling source of safety and well-being can be every bit as dangerous as uncritical trust in a nineteenth-century huckster's snake oil or a twentieth-century cult leader's immortality theories.

Sincerity isn't enough to protect us from believing or becoming illusionists. Those loyal, "permanently" relocated immortality seekers did both. First they consumed their leaders' unbiblical and illusory dogma. Then the devotees added to that illusion as they sincerely sought to persuade others to swallow it. A similar process occurs when scientists sincerely believe they can, or soon will, control lives and events "like God," and then teach students that worldview. But unintended, unrecognized, and utterly sincere illusions nevertheless remain illusions.

ILLUSION'S AMAZING ATTRACTION

We've seen that honest illusionists seek to amaze and entertain us. And deliberate deceivers try to gain a power advantage to further their hidden agendas. But why do the reasonably intelligent adults crowding the MOST PEOPLE corner of our grid tend to load their belief systems with so many illusions from the dopey to the deadly?

And since "Illusionists R Us," we need to ask ourselves: why don't *we* spot distortions of reality every time and automatically punch our mental EJECT button?

A HEART PROBLEM

"It's the economy, Stupid!" That's what the Democratic party emphasized in its successful 1992 Presidential campaign.

"It's the heart, People!" This is what our Creator God has repeated many times in many ways throughout His Word to us.

The Bible uses the word *mind* in the New Testament much the same way as *heart* in the Old. Both terms refer to that part of us that perceives and interprets information, reasons, and makes decisions. And according to Scripture, deception attracts this heart/mind of ours as surely as a magnet draws iron, because our hearts are "deceitful." (See Jeremiah 17:9 for one of the clearest statements on this issue.)

Years ago when our family lived in Seattle, we visited a salmon hatchery. Those amazing fish were literally swimming upstream against a powerful current to achieve their procreative purpose. If they had stopped struggling against the current, they would have drifted downstream and away from their species-sustaining goal.

We're like those salmon swimming upstream when we pursue truth and seek reality with our naturally deceitful hearts. The inborn drift of human reasoning inevitably carries us toward unreality and illusion. So what can we do about these deception-loving hearts and minds of ours that tend to go with the flow of magical thinking and illusory living? The answer brings us to the remaining corner of the **Illusionist Identification Grid** (Figure 3-1).

TRUTH-ANCHORED PEOPLE

The prevailing teaching of the day pictures basically good and wise, straight-thinking human beings who occasionally wander onto wrong paths. (Although in this age of limitless tolerance, we rarely hear anything labeled "wrong," short of serial killings.) And most people believe this flattering view of humankind.

Yet as we've discovered, that view of human nature contrasts totally with biblical truth. And the view one holds makes all the difference in the world when we're talking about illusions. If I believe that large vehicles traveling at high speeds cannot hit or harm my body because I am so agile and strong, I will likely walk onto a busy highway without much hesitation. That's a lot like believing our minds can instantly identify or remain unaffected by deception because we are naturally wise and straight-thinking.

Recently, I read about a white Bengal tiger that fatally mauled a zookeeper after the man mistakenly entered the animal's outdoor exhibit. In response to questions about the animal's fate, the zoo director said, "Nothing happens to the tiger. . . . [He] was just being a tiger."[8]

When we take God's view of our minds, we will recognize just being a human includes our natural, and sometimes tragic, susceptibility to deception and distortions of reality. This truth helps to forge the anchor we desperately need to keep us from drifting toward lives filled with more magical thinking, illusions, and lies.

Think about It

List some illusions you have *constructed* to increase your sense of personal safety and well-being. (Examples: If I get the corner office, or fit into a size six, I'll finally be really happy.)

List some illusions you have *consumed* that promised control over your health and longevity, financial or romantic success, etc. (Examples: This vitamin guarantees longer life, or this toothpaste makes me more kissable.)

Pray about It

DEAR LORD, I seem to have such a difficult time letting You be God. I keep looking to myself, or science, or something else to control my world. Please help me see the illusions that litter my life. Please help me be willing to agree with You about who is really in control—You. Thank You for being patient with me. AMEN.

Learn More about It

What a predicament! That line from an old movie comic accurately describes the situation we're in, doesn't it? I mean even if we manage to substantially outgrow the magical thinking of our childhood, we all have deception-friendly minds as adults.

How can we ever overcome and conquer such an enormous problem? By surrendering it, as we'll learn in chapter 4.

PART TWO:

How Do We Release Control of Our World?

FOUR

Surrendering Our Illusions of Control

"Denial is not just 'de name of a river in Egypt!"

Conference participants usually laugh when I say that in my presentations. Then the groans begin as the audience identifies with the major role denial plays in our lives. And that's no laughing matter, especially for those of us seeking to surrender our God-imitating control fantasies.

Denial sabotages efforts to escape lives marked by magical thinking and illusions of control. When denial fogs our perceptions, we can't recognize it because *the function of denial is to cloud our capacities to know we are in denial!* Only as denial lifts do we realize what it is and does.

Can you see how denial about our magical thinking and control illusions short-circuits our efforts to have more truth-based lives? We not only don't know what we *don't* know of truth, but we don't know what we *do* know and have accepted as truth. And big chunks of what we've accepted as truth may actually be magical illusions. Without insight about our accepted "truths," we'll never uncover the core beliefs that guide our thoughts and behaviors, since our magical thinking usually hides in a fog of denial.

Denial's double-bind especially troubles Christians who know that God exhorts us to "understand [our] ways," i.e., our manner of living, as He does in Proverbs 14:8. This verse — and countless others, calls us to intentionally cast off the warm, fuzzy security blanket of denial and face the often cold, prickly truth about the nature of life in general and our own lives in particular.

As we learned in chapter 2, growing up in an unhealthy family

53

tutored us to function in denial. If incongruity between reality and verbal statements about reality became commonplace, that becomes our reality. What's more, we learned in the last chapter that seeking and identifying truth presents a virtually insurmountable challenge to the deceitful hearts/minds God says we all have. (Remember the salmon swimming upstream?) So how in the world are we supposed to surrender our denial-entrenched magical thinking?

GOD'S SOLUTION TO OUR DENIAL PROBLEM

I love Psalm 51:6 because this verse specifically addresses the stumbling block of denial each of us faces when we seek to embark on a journey to truth about our unbiblical and unhealthy thinking patterns and lifestyles.

> Behold, Thou dost desire truth in the innermost being, and in the hidden part Thou wilt make me know wisdom.

Did you know you have a "hidden part" in your life that shapes your innermost being? Perhaps not, since *awareness* of your hidden part has probably been *hiding* in your hidden part! But nothing can hide from the God of truth. And He promised to give us the hidden-parts wisdom we humanly lack and desperately need. Yet, as always, God seems to give us choices.

From my experience, observation, and understanding of Scripture, I rarely see God beat us over the head with hidden-parts wisdom, ambush us with insight, or drag us kicking and screaming out of denial. Now of course, God can change us any way He wants to. That's part of His job description! Nevertheless, God appears most often to change powerfully those who open their hearts to His ongoing inspection and direction. And I believe *that* is God's solution to our denial problem. The Psalmist discovered this.

In Psalm 139:23-24, David asks God to search his heart (his innermost being) and reveal his "hurtful ways." The Psalmist knew that he lacked truthful self-knowledge, so he went to the only Source of truth — God. In Psalm 51:6 language, David asked God to give him hidden-parts wisdom about his hurtful ways.

From what the Bible reveals of David's life, we know he had

some pretty hurtful ways. And by the time he wrote Psalm 51, David knew it too. No doubt he, like many of us, longed to make significant changes in his life. And he wisely sensed that to do that, he had to know more than he knew about himself. Said differently, David wanted to rebuild some vital parts of his crumbling life, but he knew he couldn't clearly see the damage that needed repair. Nehemiah could have told David what to do.

SURVEYING DAMAGED FOUNDATIONS

In Nehemiah 2:11-18, we learn that a wise leader understood the need to take time to personally survey what's been damaged before beginning to rebuild. I believe that what was true for Jerusalem's wall is equally true for our lives.

Some of us run around frantically shoring up our crumbling lives by replacing a brick here, repairing a spot there. We're confused and discouraged because we don't experience the sense of wholeness we seek. In effect, we are attempting to rebuild our unseen, innermost being without taking the time to personally survey the damage and losses.

Typically, we accept someone else's opinion of what's wrong and needs fixing in our lives. I'm suggesting that to substantially surrender our magical thinking and crippling control fantasies, to significantly change our hurting and hurtful ways, we must ask God to direct both the damage surveying and the rebuilding processes.

Now I think we'd all agree that whether we're rebuilding city walls or life structures, we must accurately assess damage to the foundations. In both cases, as the foundation goes, so goes the subsequent structure. Of course, since foundations are usually buried out of sight, realistically surveying them usually requires some digging.

Those of us seeking to unearth truth about the foundations of our fantasy-plagued lives should not be too surprised when family-instilled denial and human self-deceit get in the way. That's why we must ask God to give us wisdom about the foundations of our innermost beings that usually lie underground, in our "hidden parts" out of our awareness. Obviously, since foundations refer to the earliest part of any building project, that means we'll be looking at the families into which we were born.

Now there's a sentence that can shoot our anxiety levels right through the roof!

FEARS ABOUT LOOKING AT
OUR FOUNDATIONS

Family of origin trauma. Toxic parents. Adult children of _____ (fill in the blank). Are you weary of the parent and family bashing so prevalent in print and broadcast media? Me too.

Yet, no matter how much we resist the notion, the truth remains that the families into which we were born served as our earliest, most influential education institution. So, when we seek to understand why some of us struggle with prolonged magical thinking more than others, we need to take an honest look at our childhood experiences.

That's not bashing. That's reality. And for many of us, that's also distressing. It sure was for Mike.

"Just because God tells us to have truth in our innermost whatever and to understand why we do what we do, doesn't mean we should look at our parents' past treatment of us. I refuse to drive my life by looking in the rearview mirror!" Those were Mike's comments to me during a coffee break at a Christian conference where I had talked about what we're discussing in this chapter.

Obviously agitated, Mike rushed on to asked a crucial question. "Why look back anyway? Doesn't Paul talk about forgetting the past in Phillipians? I think that's what God really wants us to do. Just forget all that _____ (deleted expletive)!" Afraid he'd offended me I suppose, Mike apologized for using the word I deleted from his comments.

I wasn't especially offended, but I certainly was amazed by the anger that oozed into this young Christian's face and voice as he spoke of the past he thought he should "just forget." And I wondered if Mike frequently struggled with anger contaminating his communication and relationships without any clue that it stemmed, in part, from early family problems.

I wondered because that's what often happens when people are unwilling to look back at an obviously painful past. They get stuck in a pain-filled present. Sometimes they get stuck in sadness or fear rather than anger. If so, they're apt to get prescriptions for antidepressants or tranquilizers. And if they *do* get stuck in anger, like Mike, those nearest and dearest to them will likely be taking the antidepressants and/or tranquilizers!

Now it is absolutely true that we are not to make decisions and run our lives based on our emotions. That approach guarantees constant chaos, if not downright disaster. However, it is also true that our feelings—especially the prevailing emotion that pops out frequently in distressing ways—reveal what's going on in our belief systems. And that's pretty helpful, since many of us don't have a clue about the foundational beliefs on which we have built our lives. In other words, our prevailing unpleasant emotions function sort of like the warning lights on the dashboard of a car. They let us know what's going on inside. Or to use our building simile, those prevalent, distressing feelings are like spreading cracks in the structure of our lives. They indicate problems somewhere in the foundation.

There was no way I could know with complete certainty what was going on inside Mike. But I could see that Mike's sincere attempts to forget his apparently distressing childhood did not seem to bring the personal and spiritual peace he deeply desired. Mike felt stuck, in part because he feared the foundation-surveying process that would have provided helpful information for the personal rebuilding he desired.

Christians who want to avoid this necessary early foundation-surveying task often quote Bible verses out of context to support their positions. Mike did that when he referred to "Paul in Philippians." Let's look at two "forgetting" verses that are frequently used to teach a kind of selective and sanctified amnesia about parental influence in childhood. (It's selective because we're supposed to remember only the *happy* times.)

SCRIPTURE AND "FORGETTING"

In Philippians 3:13 Paul says he is *"forgetting what lies behind and reaching forward to what lies ahead."* Is he telling us to blot out recollection of everything, or the unpleasant things, about our birth families and the past in general? We find the answer to this important question when we place verse thirteen in proper context by reading verses four through twelve.

In that section of Scripture we learn that Paul had an extremely specific forgetting in mind. He was forgetting all the religious heritage and accomplishment he once used to establish his right standing with God. Paul clearly did not mean he couldn't recall those things because he does exactly that in verses four through six. Rather, in "forgetting" those things he set them aside and/or viewed them differently than he did before he met Christ. In Genesis 41:51 Joseph talked about forgetting when he explained the meaning of his first son's name. Joseph named the baby boy Manasseh because *"God has made me forget all my trouble and all my father's household."* Again, this is a special kind of forgetting that does not include pretending that unpleasant childhood experiences never happened. We see that clearly in Genesis 50:20 when Joseph bluntly reminds his long-lost brothers, "You meant evil against me."

So what did Joseph mean when he used the word "forget" in Genesis 41:51? We get a clue to the answer when Joseph explains his second son's name in the next verse: "And he named the second [son] Ephraim, 'For,' he said, 'God has made me fruitful in the land of my affliction.' " If Joseph had nursed a bitter resentment about his brothers' mistreatment, he would never have had such a clear sense of God's abundant blessing in his life. Now, we know Joseph could, and did, recall the sibling abuse. So the kind of forgetting Joseph said God caused apparently removed the stinging *pain* of childhood mistreatment without eliminating the *truth* about it.

Now, please understand. I am not saying we should have past-focused lives of self-absorbed "navel-gazing." (Neither Paul nor Joseph did, and Nehemiah certainly didn't spend his life simply strolling through the rubble of Jerusalem's walls.) On the contrary, we look back at the early influences that shaped our beliefs and choices in order to sort through the confusing tangle of fantasy and facts *for the very purpose of moving forward and wisely rebuilding our lives.*

Christians, especially those of us who know or suspect that we grew up in pretty unhealthy homes, face another fear related to looking back at our family foundations. Many of us fear that if we honestly face our pasts, we will be dishonoring our parents. It seems so much easier just to say that what our folks did or failed to do didn't really affect us that much anyway. Ironically, *that's* precisely the attitude that dishonors our parents.

FEARS ABOUT DISHONORING OUR PARENTS

Most of us know we have been commanded to honor our parents in Exodus 20:12. But few of us know what honor actually means as conveyed by the Hebrew language in which that commandment was written. We may be a lot like Angie.

"I was always taught, 'If you can't say anything nice don't say anything at all' when it came to how you talk about people. Especially family members. The idea of letting myself talk or even think honestly about some of the less-than-nice stuff that went on when I was a kid scares me to death!" That's how Angie, a Christian in her early forties, described her anxiety about looking at the childhood environment that shaped her beliefs and choices. Angie's confusion about how to reconcile honesty and honoring cleared when she learned about one Hebrew word.

The word translated *honor* in Exodus 20:12 originally referred to something of great weight. Over time the word began to be used about important individuals, like city officials or judges, who were considered "weighty" because of their heavy influence in the community.[1]

Clearly, the Hebrew word for honor suggests a far different attitude toward parents than most of us have been taught. But when you stop to think about it, isn't God's directive to truthfully assess the weight of our parents' heavy influences in our lives consistent with His emphasis on us having truth in our innermost beings? To do otherwise would dishonor our parents and misrepresent the character of God who always condemns deception and extols truth.

About now you may be thinking, "All right, Sandy, I'm beginning to see that maybe I'd be wise to look at some of the foundational influences that shaped my beliefs and choices. There's just one more thing that bothers me about all this foundation-surveying stuff. I don't want to end up sounding like a candidate for 'Oprah.' You know, one of those people always whining about how her parents are to blame for everything that's going wrong in her life." Good point.

FEARS ABOUT BLAMING VERSUS PERSONAL RESPONSIBILITY

If you've ever listened to an adult on some talk show blaming his or her parents or other authority figure for ruining his or her life, you probably wanted to yell, "Grow up!" As my husband can verify, I've done exactly that more than once.

Indeed, growing up in the fullest sense includes taking personal responsibility for our lives. Certainly, we must attribute realistic responsibility to our parents' heavy influences in shaping our early choices. But now that we are adults, *we—not our parents—must take full responsibility for our choices and our lives.*

Using personal power terminology, our parents will always *influence* us. That is an appropriate and realistic use of a parent's personal power in relationships with adult offspring. But in reality, our parents no longer have the personal power to *control* the perceptions of life that molded our choices as they did when we were children.

Can you see that honestly evaluating the early influences that may have helped to prolong our magical thinking does not mean we must play a blame game? And can you also recognize the wisdom of honestly surveying the damage in the foundations of our belief systems before starting to rebuild? If so, we're ready to turn an important corner to examine a blueprint for rebuilding truth-founded belief systems and lifestyles substantially free from magical illusions of control.

A BLUEPRINT FOR TRUTH-BASED LIVING

Nearly everyone has heard of the "three *R's*": Reading, (w)Riting, and (a)Rithmetic. I believe there are five *R's* that will provide a kind of blueprint to guide our life-rebuilding efforts. They are: (1) Release, (2) Reflect, (3) Review, (4) Restructure, and (5) Rely. Each of those *R* words begins a statement that summarizes the five parts of a changing/ rebuilding process. Let's take a closer look at them.

1. RELEASE our lives and our changing processes to God by asking Him to take control of both.

You will remember that in the last chapter we identified a serious problem in our hearts/minds: they naturally incline toward deceit. Obviously, that problem will obstruct the path to more truthful living. Obviously too, if we have a heart/mind problem, we need a heart/mind solution. And that is precisely what God promises those who accept His diagnosis of their sin-diseased hearts.

The Gospels unfold the details of this divine heart transplant. The Great Physician, Jesus—who is God wrapped in bones and skin—repeatedly tells us about this fatal heart defect in verses such as Mark 7:21. He says we cannot treat this terminal condition ourselves because it is caused by something we carry within — our sin.

Specifically, Jesus says we need a new birth to get a new heart. In the language of John 3:16, God loves us so much He provided the outside intervention required to cure our fatal heart disease by putting on a cloak of flesh and taking all of our sin-sickness on Himself. When we choose to trust in the *eternally* life-saving effectiveness of that awesome sacrifice, we become His children and the heart/mind changing process begins.[2]

Accepting God's divine heart transplant requires us to do what any of us who have had surgery in a hospital have had to do. We intentionally surrendered our attempts to control our problems, and we released ourselves into the hands of the surgical team. In fact, I remember signing a *release* form.

Now I realize I'm mixing medical and construction imagery here. But I think we have to, in effect, sign a release form to give control of ourselves and our life-restructuring to God. As I understand Scripture, we do that by asking Jesus to be Savior and Lord.

God sends His Holy Spirit to live within us to produce truth-based and Christlike changes in us because our changed lives bring glory to God. This reality means that God has a stake in our changing/healing efforts all along the way, not just at the first step. But that doesn't remove *our* purposeful and persistent responsibility in this life-rebuilding process. Our part includes (at least) the four remaining *R's* in our blueprint for change. And we'll surely require divine assistance at number two.

2. REFLECT on the prevailing patterns of our lives to identify foundational beliefs.

It may seem strange that I don't simply say we ought to identify our core beliefs. But as you've learned by now, I doubt many of us can recognize those beliefs unless we've asked God to help us genuinely, consistently turn our backs on magical thinking to pursue truth. The repeated choices that shape our lives may not match what we profess, but they always reveal what we believe.

For example, we may profess to believe the biblical truth that being a Christian doesn't mean we are perfect. Yet our lives, and the lives of those close to us, may bear the marks of bondage to life-crushing perfectionism. Believing we must be perfect blasts a hole through the foundation of our lives. Trying to patch the collapsing structure over that hole won't do much good without some major repair work on the faulty foundation. And foundation level work leads us to the third *R* word: *review.*

3. REVIEW the foundational beliefs we learned as truth in our birth families.

I've spent a lot of time building a case for the critical importance of this step. At the risk of belaboring the point, I want to emphasize again the power birth families exert in all our lives.

Our late childhood, adolescent, and adult beliefs and choices form the structure of our lives. But the foundation was laid in early childhood by the interaction of our experiences and our immature, magical thinking. Our families defined truth with a capital *T.* And those family-defined truths may or may not have been based on reality. Either way, we really had no choice as kids except to grab hold of them and build them into the foundations of our lives where they're apt to remain hidden from our view. That's why we need to re-view, literally look again at, what we learned to believe as true.

This re-view and sorting of foundational beliefs sounds like an integral part of something the Apostle Paul mentioned in 1 Corinthians 13:11. In that verse, Paul talks about "putting away childish things," specifically childish words, thoughts, and ways of reasoning. How could we separate the childish thoughts that we need to put away from thoughts that are mature and need to be retained if we don't uncover what we learned to think and believe in childhood? And this process of re-viewing and evaluating of foundational beliefs opens the door to our next rebuilding task.

4. RESTRUCTURE our beliefs and behaviors based on truth instead of magical thinking and illusions of control.

Recently, I've studied the Hebrew and Greek meanings of *truth* as used in the Old and New Testaments.[3] Two distinct but overlapping concepts emerge. Most biblical scholars agree that the Greek sense of truth means the reality, the genuine essence of a matter, in contrast to its surface appearance. In other words, truth stands in opposition to falsehood, concealment, distortion, deception, or delusion. The Hebrew concept of truth conveys faithfulness, stability, and reliability. I believe that learning to identify and believe what is true, as opposed to what is false, and then choosing appropriate responses to that truth forms the core of our life restructuring process. And more truth-filled belief systems produce more stable lives.

Clearly, I am saying that the nature of one's *thought* life determines the nature of one's *entire* life, which admittedly is a pretty sweeping statement. Actually, I'm in the best possible company asserting this. God tells us that thinking determines life in Proverbs 23:7: "... for as [a person] thinks within himself, so he is." (And *she* is too.) Just imagine — how I think determines who I am. Talk about a sweeping statement! No wonder God repeatedly insists on us having truth in our hearts/minds where our thinking originates.

In Romans 12:2, God describes His plan for our personal restructuring from people who lean toward deceit into people who live in truth. God calls this restructuring process *transformation.* In that verse, the Greek verb tense indicates continuous action.[4] A literal translation is, "... but keep on being transformed by the continuous renewing of your mind. ..." These words describe an ongoing, lifelong process rather than a one time event.

I don't know about you, but I get worried and weary just *hearing* about an "ongoing, lifelong process," let alone *committing* to one. I prefer projects that are fast and finished.

5. RELY on God's faithfulness, not our own.

All-or-nothing thinking perfectionists like me expect to flawlessly master this mind-renewal business, achieve total transformation, and be done with it. This sort of unrealistic reasoning sabotages our pursuit of truthful living when we encounter lingering evidence of deceitful thinking. *And we always do.*

We need to remember that our assurance of genuine, eternally significant change rests not in our own abilities to perfectly discern deception and follow truth. Our confidence rests in God's faithfulness to keep His promises.

For example, Jesus promised His followers they would receive the Holy Spirit, the power source they needed to help them remember His teachings and live for Him. (See John 14:26.) And knowing that believers would get confused about who assumes the primary responsibility for supervising and energizing their inner transformations, God spells it out in Philippians 1:6.

> Being confident of this, that [God] who began a good work in you will carry it on to completion until the day of Christ Jesus.

As Christians, our confident hope of being transformed by the renewing of our minds rests securely in God the Father, Son, and Holy Spirit's faithfulness to promises like these. That's why this five-part model begins and ends with the focus on God. After all, Hebrews 12:2 calls Jesus the author and finisher of our faith.

God also wants to be our stronghold.

SURRENDERING FALSE STRONGHOLDS

In this chapter I've used construction imagery as we looked at the need to survey foundations and restructure our belief systems. But as I consider my own continuing struggle to live in truth, and the struggles of those with whom I've counseled, I conclude that something more is going on inside us.

Our hearts and minds resemble a battlefield more than a building site. Changing lifelong patterns of thinking requires warfare, not just re-modeling. The old, false stronghold must come down so a new and true place of safety can be established.

A stronghold is a fortress, a place of safety and refuge. In 2 Corinthians 10:4-5 we learn that each of us has a false stronghold in our minds, specifically a thought system that "sets itself up against the knowledge of God" (NIV). Trying to be like God by living as if we can completely control our lives and relationships sounds to me like a major fortification in this "against-the-knowledge-of-God" mental stronghold. No wonder these verses tell us only divine weapons can tear it down so we can "take captive every thought to make it obedient to Christ" (NIV).

The Psalmist discovered that God is our only sure stronghold and true source of safety. He shared that life-changing truth with us in verses like Psalm 62:6:

> He only is my rock and my salvation, My stronghold;
> I shall not be shaken.

God asks us to surrender our childhood stronghold of magical thinking with its protective illusions of control and safety. God understands that this challenging, if not terrifying, task lasts a lifetime. So when we grow weary from the struggle against deception, He wants us to remember to find our refuge in Him.

Think about It

Are you willing to survey the foundations of your life to discover damage in your childhood perceptions and current beliefs? If so, will you ask God to give you wisdom in your inner "hidden part"? If not, why not?

You take the most important and absolutely essential step toward surrendering illusions of control when you ask Jesus into your life to take control. If you have never done that, you can do it right now by praying something like the prayer below. Remember, these are not magical words. God cares about the true intentions of your heart, not the form of your prayer.

If you have already asked Jesus to be your Savior and Lord, reaffirm your desire to let Him have control of your life.

Pray about It

DEAR LORD, You know how hard it is for me to give up control of anything, let alone my life and eternal destiny. But I am choosing to believe Your promise to cleanse me of sin, make me Your beloved child, and transform my life. Please come into my heart to be my Savior and my Lord. Thank You for dying for me to make this possible. AMEN.

Learn More about It

Whether you are a brand-new Christian or an old-timer like me, you likely want to think and live in more mature and stable ways. And, like me, you may read self-help books, talk to friends, and/or seek pastoral or professional counseling from time to time to produce these changes.

In the next chapter we will discover that the illusions of control we long to correct have a way of contaminating the very methods we use to correct them.

Magical Fixes, Change, and Counseling

"Diet Magic."

That magazine ad headline sure grabbed my attention. I barely managed to resist ordering the magical, guaranteed weight-loss pills. Whether it's losing excess pounds, controlling destructive habits, or changing our thinking and living patterns, we all long for magical fixes.

Christians, too, seek the anointed zaps of sanctified magic. After all, we don't stop being human when we start being a Christian. And human beings seem to naturally pursue self-deceptive shortcuts, i.e., illegitimate means to legitimate ends.

In this chapter, we will examine some of the fantasy fixes we're apt to pursue when we live with magical thinking. And as we do, we'll discover that help*ers* can succumb to illusions of control as easily as help*ees*. Let's begin with the fantasy fixes often sought by those of us seeking changes in our lives.

FANTASY FIXES FOR MAGICAL CHANGE

When you stop to think about it, it makes sense that distressed, hurting, confused people would be suckers for magical methods of producing the changes they desire in their relationships and lives. I've identified four of the most common fantasy fixes. As you read about them, you may recognize yourself. Please don't become discouraged or embarassed. We live what we've learned even when we seek to change the way we live.

1. The Solely Spiritual Fix

Some sincere Christians seem to believe that human beings are only *spiritual* beings, so they teach that *human* problems are solely *spiritual* problems. When pressed, they may add the physical component to human nature and struggles. But nothing more.

These believers usually validate their opinions by asserting their devotion to Scripture. I find that ironic since Genesis 1:26-27 says that God created human beings "in His own image." Of course God is supremely spiritual. But He is more. In Scripture and most clearly in Jesus, we see that God also has thinking, feeling, and relating aspects to His nature; therefore, as creatures made in God's image, we also have those qualities.

When the original image bearers "fell," every aspect of God's image in human beings was shattered, virtually beyond recognition. We see sin's pervasive effects in our disease and decay-prone physical bodies. We also see them in the invisible rational, emotional, relational, and spiritual aspects of us that reflect God's image. We know that sin's spiritual impact on us caused a deadly separation from God. Why should we be surprised that the past and present effects of sin, both ours and others, create problems in our thinking, feeling, and relating?

I think too many Christians have been taught what amounts to a magic trick: making intellectual, emotional, and relational natures and struggles appear to vanish. Unfortunately, that's just an illusion. And creating illusions requires deception, whereas God deals in truth. Christians seeking solely-spiritual fixes usually belong to churches that consider seeing a counselor evidence that the counselee doesn't trust the sufficiency of Christ. (Of course some churches hold the same view when it comes to seeing a physician.)

The most strident counseling critics within Christendom often ask sarcastically how believers managed to cope centuries ago before psychospouting therapists infiltrated the church. One might just as reasonably ask how believers made it without modern medicine and physicians. Perhaps the answer to both questions is the same: often very painfully. After recently unearthing the bodies of seventeenth-century pilgrims, that's the clear conclusion researchers drew about the lack of skilled medical services for debilitating physical problems routinely solved nowadays. The pilgrims' bodies revealed that they lived very short, pain-filled lives.

I think it is no more ungodly to see a wise, Christian counselor than it is to seek skilled medical care. Of course, if we fall into the hands of inept, unskilled, or unscrupulous counselors or medical quacks, we can experience great harm. But if we consistently seek and follow God's guidance, go to the right helpers, and prayerfully consider making the changes they suggest, we may in many respects be more fully the people God created us to be in every part of our image-bearing natures.

2. The Familiar Fix

This approach to change really puts the spotlight on us and our efforts to bring new results from knowing more, doing better, and trying harder what we've already known, done, and tried. Talk about fantasy! Essentially, we demand that God use ways that feel familiar and safe because that reduces the anxiety we experience when the unfamiliar makes us feel out-of-control.

How does this work out in real life? Readers will try to read more and better books. Spiritualizers will spend more time in devotions and at church. Socializers may start attending support or therapy groups. Or attending *more* of them. Thinkers are apt to seek extremely cognitive therapy that focuses exclusively on correcting misbeliefs. (It might be scary to get into all those messy emotions. It might feel too out-of-control.) Emoters, on the other hand, often gravitate toward helpers with large boxes of tissues.

Now, I'm inclined to think that most of us would benefit by all of the above. Books, private and corporate worship, and Christ-centered groups all have a place in our changing processes. And by now you know how critical I think it is to identify and correct misbeliefs, including those that keep us in emotional straightjackets. God has demonstrated His willingness to use astoundingly diverse means of instruction and blessing in the lives of His children. Part of our healing from the effects of control fantasies involves yielding control to God to orchestrate our changing processes according to His perfect knowledge of us. Obviously, that's a pretty terrifying prospect for many of us magical-thinking over-controllers.

Part of our problem lies in the fact that those of us who grew up in unhealthy families lack some basic living skills to one degree or another. We naturally are drawn to those activities that are familar because we feel competent and comfortable there. We usually avoid those where we don't.

Part of my most recent counseling included experiences intended to help me learn to rest, relax, and take better care of myself. All of those things were way out of my comfort zone since I am far more familiar with overwork, tension, and self-neglect. That's right. I sought some additional counseling within the past year even though I have worked a lot on my "stuff" on and off through the years. Obviously, I've learned that changing does not include quick fixes despite all my magical-thinking otherwise.

3. The Quick Fix

"Instant Improvement, Inc." said the return address on the large envelope I recently received. In brilliant red print, the envelope proclaimed, "She fled the hospital when the doctor said, 'Cut her open.' but in one night, these New Generation Healers simply flushed out her disease." (I am *not* making this up.) I decided not to buy the expensive volume detailing the hospital-escapee's amazing saga. But believe me, I was tempted, especially since I could also learn about (I'm quoting directly here) "lightning-fast cures" for nearly every conceivable physical ailment known to medical science. (Lest you get the wrong impression of my ability to resist quick-fix pitches, you need to know that I once purchased—on sale at least—a book titled *Habit Control in a Day!*)

Nearly all of us who long to make positive changes in our lives also *long* to keep it *short*. The distance from where we are to where we want to be, that is. And we have a virtually unlimited smorgasbord of things promising to leap-frog us through the change process.

Recently, the popular media have highlighted the nearly magical personality altering power of the prescription drug, Prozac. In a February 7, 1994 feature story on Prozac, *Newsweek* magazine's cover included these enticing words to prospective readers: "Shy? Forgetful? Anxious? Fearful? Obsessed? How Science Will Let You Change Your Personality with a Pill."

But not all mental health professionals have boarded the pro-Prozac bandwagon. In an article subtitled "Doctor Fears Any 'Quick Fixes,' " internationally reknowned psychiatrist Oliver Sacks warned about the dangers of using Prozac and similar medications to provide "the made-to-order personality of your choice."[1] Sacks' concerns come from his 1960s experiments with the drug L-dopa, used to treat survivors of a 1920s sleeping sickness epidemic. Patients were initially revived by the drug, only to slip back into a stupor. Dr. Sacks documented his experiences in the book *Awakenings.*

If you don't want to take pills, you can always sign up for some program or another. Maybe it's a three-day conference, a four-part Bible study, or a ten-week group. Whatever it is, we want to believe that at the end of the three days, the four parts, or ten weeks, there will be a new, improved version of us who doesn't have to struggle with all the tedious, tiring, sometimes terrifying aspects of making and practicing the new choices that bring change.

Pills and programs seem to give us a handle to manage, read that—*control,* our change efforts. But committing to truth confronts us with the reality of a process perspective, as we discovered in the last chapter. In fact, process will be a recurring theme throughout this book. Adopting a process perspective regarding change means that, not only will we expect it to take time, but we'll be prepared for some loose ends. And that's unwelcome news for us magical thinkers who insist on total fixes.

4. The Total Fix

It seems to me that this change-process-thing is a lot like packaging a live octopus. Just about the time you think you have it all wrapped-up, something else pops out! That reality is neither appealing nor comforting to those of us susceptible to illusions of control. We tend to seek answers that are not only fast, but neat, tidy, and total as well. I think this very human desire manifests itself in two demands: no struggles and no scars.

THE DEMAND FOR NO STRUGGLES

I feel very virtuous when I recycle aluminum cans or newspapers. I feel like a failure when I recycle personal problems. After all, it's one thing to discover yet another area of my belief system that needs correcting. It is something altogether different to find myself struggling again with an issue I thought I had thoroughly dealt with already. I mean I expected change to include some struggles. I just didn't realize they would be the *same* struggles over and over. And over!

I think our individual struggles come from the interaction of our sin natures, our unique genetic endowments, and the childhood experiences that shaped our character development. Since I've told you a little about myself, you probably won't be too surprised to learn that many of my ongoing personal and relational struggles revolve around father loss and abandonment issues, with a tendency toward depression thrown in to complete the picture.

As I mentioned earlier, within the past year I went to a wonderful Christian woman[2] for additional counseling to deal with a recurring sense of sadness I was leaking all over my family and friends. I have known this counselor for several years and had done some training with her. About a year ago, I attended an advanced training weekend under her direction, during which time I had two therapy session (as did each of the other two trainees) as part of the instruction. My sadness "leak" became a gusher. And I knew I needed to schedule a week with her to give myself the gift of time and opportunity to do the deep grieving so obviously needed.

When I went for my six days of intensive (four hours a day) therapy, I knew that I did not need to uncover more memories of childhood trauma. Instead, I needed a safe place away from routine responsibilities, and a trustworthy person to guide me as I finally let myself grieve childhood losses, particularly the father I never knew. You see, God had used the tender, joyful, loving relationship so readily apparent between my son and my granddaughter to tap into that soul-deep pool of pain and grief from my father-loss.

Believe me, it was difficult to give myself permission to take my emotional struggles seriously enough to spend the time and money it took to go. "After all," I told myself, "you've already worked on your issues. You understand all this. You've written books about this stuff and helped others with this sort of thing. You shouldn't be having these emotional struggles."

I'm so grateful that I listened to the gentle nudgings of the Holy Spirit rather than the "you-should-be-over-this" part of me. Am I saying I think you ought to go for counseling? Or for more counseling? I don't know you well enough to say that. But I *am* saying that the demand for total fixes with no loose ends and no ongoing struggles is Fantasyland living. So is the demand for wounds without scars.

THE DEMAND FOR NO SCARS

Throughout my years as a counselor and conference speaker, I have been asked one question perhaps more than any other. It comes in different forms, but they are all variations on the same theme: "when will I be able to live as if it never happened?"

That deep longing expresses the unrealistic desire, even demand, for wounds to heal without scars. On my left forearm, I have a scar from a biopsy that was performed nearly twenty-five years ago. That surgical wound has been healed for two-and-a-half decades. Yet, I have a scar that bears witness to the therapeutic trauma my flesh sustained so long ago.

Scars — noticeable evidence of significant wounds or injuries — are not admissions of healing failure. Scars speak to the reality of human woundability not only in our visible, physical selves, but also in our unseen rational, emotional, relational, and spiritual natures. They challenge our longing to control the effects of living in a sin-broken world as, and with, sin-broken people. Scars call us to more realistic expectations of recovery in the presence of sin.

Obviously, I am suggesting that no matter how much counseling we receive or self-help energy we expend, we're still going to face struggles and see "scars" that reveal past pain. So that raises a very important question. What are we going to do with these struggles and scars? Hide them? Blame them on our potty training? I think that, as Christians who have a steadfast hope and an eternal future, we instead can learn from them and grow in the midst of them.

Of course, we can also blame our ongoing struggles and obvious emotional/relational scars on our decidedly imperfect helpers. And some of us who harbor colossally unrealistic expectations of them do just that. Few of us, however, will ever have more magical illusions about our helpers than they are apt to have about themselves.

MAGICAL-THINKING COUNSELING MODELS

So, now that we've seen some of the magical fixes helpees commonly seek, let's look at a few of the typical illusions cherished (discreetly, of course) by many helpers. These fantasies manifest themselves in the counseling models magically-thinking helpers follow.

1. The Cookie-cutter Confrontation Model

"Take two Quiet Times and call me in the morning" captures the essence of this approach which is the counseling model of choice for helpers who see all counseling issues as solely spiritual.

Christian counselors who practice from this perspective frequently focus primarily on confronting counselees' sins. In fact, a kind of cookie-cutter confrontational style is used regardless of the counselee's issues. These well-meaning people helpers nearly always use the Bible to bolster their "stop-that-start-this" model of counseling. Too bad they somehow missed one of the important lessons taught in the actions of Jesus and the words of the apostle Paul.

Jesus' Individualized Approach
I don't know about you, but if I had perfected a method to heal blind people, I think I'd stick with it. But Jesus didn't. In Matthew 9:27-31, we read that Jesus heals two blind men instantly. Whereas in Mark 8:22-26, stages of progressive healing seem to be involved. And in John 9:1-7 we see the spit-and-clay method. Now, I don't know why Jesus didn't just repeat the same technique with all the blind people He healed. The point is that He didn't.

In 1 Thessolonians 5:14, the Holy Spirit of God, via the Apostle Paul, provides more direct instructions to people helpers with an appetite for cookie-cutter approaches. In that verse, Paul urges believers to do four things as they interact with one another:
(1) admonish the unruly,
(2) encourage the fainthearted,
(3) help the weak; and
(4) be patient with all men (and I assume with all women also).

Clearly, we see that people helpers are to avoid dealing with everyone in the same confrontive manner. Clearly too, some folks, i.e., the "unruly," benefit when helpers admonish/confront them about the consequences of their unwise choices.

While some helpers seem to believe they have the gift of confrontation, others have difficulty admonishing even the most self-destructive and unruly person. To insure the appreciative devotion of those we're helping, we might indulge in a kind of conspicuous compassion that comes more from our own brokenness than our biblical convictions.

74

Jesus did not display unlimited tolerance for ungodly behavior. Neither should contemporary helpers, despite our culture's prevailing live-and-let-live philosophy. What's more, just because some of the people who seek our help have been deeply hurt does not exempt them from being personally responsible when they hurt themselves or others. This attitude of personal responsibility reflects genuine, godly love rather than the "sloppy *agape*" that shrugs and winks at wrong.

Becoming an adept admonisher isn't enough to be a truly helpful helper since the "fainthearted" and "weak" need encouragement and help instead. And I love the fact that that verse validates a process perspective to helping people by instructing us to "be patient with all. . . ." So whatever problem helpees present, helpers are to have an attitude that includes patience. We don't need patience when something is simple and quick, do we? Patience speaks to ongoing process. What an important reminder for all people helpers, whether pastor, mental health professional, lay-counselor, or dear friend.

If we helpers have been stamping out the same, confrontive counseling style, we need to toss out our cookie-cutters. The sooner the better. In their place, we need to practice prayerfully individualized helping within the parameters of our knowledge, experience, and skills. That's a pretty unnerving thought for many of us helpers because, like the people who seek our assistance, we're apt to feel most comfortable and in control when we stick to the familiar.

2. The Feels-familiar Counseling Model

Someone has observed that *if the only tool we have is a hammer, we will see every problem as a nail.* Couple that truth with the reality that to some degree or another all our adult relationships are family re-unions, and we can begin to understand the special temptations facing people helpers from unhealthy families.

Anecdotal evidence suggests that those of us who grew up playing the "Hero" role in dysfunctional families flock into all types of helping professions in disproportionate numbers. It's as if we say to ourselves, "I spent my childhood trying to make my family's problems disappear, now I'll spend my adult life trying to make your problems disappear."

So the "Little Magician" grows up to become the "Mini-Messiah," while the infantile, grandiose, rescue fantasies remain unchanged.

When we operate from this magical-thinking perspective, each new helping situation gives us a chance to improve our imaginary controlling skills to make it come out different *this* time. In essence, if we haven't gained any understanding about our illusion-laden "ways" (see Proverbs 14:8) and surrendered our control fantasies, our adult helping efforts will be more about reworking our childhood failures to fix our folks and families than about ministering to those who seek our help.

I believe that unhelped helpers, i.e., those who have never received help for *their* problems, are less helpful than they might be. In fact, they can be downright dangerous. At the least, they perpetuate and validate some of the unrealistic, magical expectations helpees bring to them — including the desire for fast, total fixes.

3. The Quick-and-Total-Healing Counseling Model

Helpers are trafficking in magic when we expect deeply wounded people to respond to promises of God's redemptive purposes with instantaneous joy and totally transformed lives. Reactions more often are similar to those of the Israelites described in Exodus 6:9. That verse says that when Moses reported God's promised freedom and His choice of the Israelites as His own people, they did not listen to Moses because of "their despondency," "discouragement" (NIV), "anguish of spirit" (KJV), and "cruel bondage."

Wounds take time to heal, whether they are physical, emotional, or spiritual. *Deep wounds take longer.* And as we've already discussed, some wounds leave more noticeable scars than others. This means that some of the folks we've helped will still exhibit obvious problems even when we've done our best and prayed our hardest for them.

As wise and genuinely caring helpers, we must be willing to recognize the limits of our knowledge and skill. And we must be willing to refer when we recognize that people need *more* than our best. If we have not dealt sufficiently with our own rescue fantasies about being all-healing with all people, we'll likely resist referring.

People helpers have no magic wands to make problems disappear. (If they did, there wouldn't be so many divorced marriage counselors!) They are more like travel agents. Travel agents cannot "travel" anyone any more than helpers can heal or fix anyone. But as individuals plan and work seriously toward change, helpers can make suggestions that may favorably influence the journey.

As people helpers of whatever kind, we must remember that no matter how many funny little letters we have behind our names, we remain only *influencers,* not *controllers.* (Ph.D. does not stand for People-helping Deity!) Ideally, Christian counselors, whether professional or not, will recognize that we are messengers, not messiahs; contemporary voices, not the final word. *And acknowledging this is not saintly humility; it is simply reality!*

> I believe that Christian counseling is, more than anything else, private lessons in applied theology.

This means that I have the privilege of working with the only two things on this planet that will last forever: human beings and the Word of God. This also means that when I drift back into my besetting rescue fantasies, I work hard to focus on the real power source for change. Zechariah 4:6 states it about as well as any verse I know. As I often do with God's promises, I like to personalize this verse to help me grab hold of it. When I do, it reads like this:

> . . . This is the word of the LORD to Sandy saying, "Not by might nor by power, but by My Spirit," says the LORD of hosts.

For helpers and helpees alike, that verse provides needed commentary about the value of books, groups, counselors, physicians, pastors, and other sources of human help. Whether our issues are physical or non-physical, we always fare best when we recognize that our ultimate help and our power to change comes from the One who was called both Great Physician and Wonderful Counselor.

Think about It

If you have recognized some problems in your life, are you willing to consider the possibility that there may be more than *only* a spiritual component to them? (REMEMBER: all problems have *some* spiritual aspects.)

If you are not willing to consider this possibility, please consider re-reading the Gospels to see how Jesus ministered to more than people's spiritual problems, although that was always the most important part of His ministry.

If you are willing to see your problems as more than *only* a spiritual problem, check which one or more aspects of your humanity is/are involved:

—— physical: headaches, stomach problems, insufficient exercise, etc.
—— rational: confusion about influence versus control, etc.
—— emotional: frequent angry outbursts, recurring depression, etc.
—— relational: repeated conflicts with family members, co-workers, etc.

What resources can you identify to help you address the various aspects of your problem? Will you use those resources to get help? If so, when? If not, why not?

Pray about It

DEAR LORD, You understand far better than I how easily I fall for magical fixes. I dread the hard work and unforeseen consequences of changing. Help me to remember that You often let human helpers participate in the life-changing only You can produce. Please help me know if that is part of Your plan for me at this time. AMEN.

Learn More about It

These days many Christians and non-Christians alike buy books, attend seminars, and/or enter counseling to change what is commonly called "low self-esteem." In the following chapter, we'll discover that magical thinking's illusions of control play a major role in the critical issue of self-concept.

PART THREE:

Letting Go of Our World,
Piece by Piece

SIX

Illusions of Control,
Shame, and Perfectionism

Cause of death: control fantasies and shame.

No, that's not what twenty-two-year-old Christy Henrich's death certificate stated. The official cause was "multiple organ failure." But behind that terse explanation lies the reality of shame and control illusions.[1]

One of America's top gymnasts, Henrich missed the 1988 Olympic Team by .118 of a point. That same year, four-foot-eleven, ninety-five pound Henrich was told by a U.S. gymnastics judge that she was too fat. That comment convinced Christy that what she already had begun to believe was true. She didn't beat the top-ranked American and European gymnasts only because she wasn't as pencil-thin as they. Never mind the reality that her body was naturally more muscular. Already a compulsive calorie counter, Christy began her descent into the life-dominating eating disorder that, six years later, would take her to fifty-two pounds and death.

Christy Henrich represents an extreme example of the destructive potential of magical thinking. Throughout this chapter, I will refer to Christy's story with descriptions of her pursuit of perfect control and quotations from people close to her. We will see how Christy's magical thinking fed a sense of shame that, coupled with her control fantasies, proved fatal.

Why use such an admittedly dramatic example? I think that most of us who struggle with magical thinking's shame-shaped perceptions find it nearly impossible to recognize the *subtle* manifestations. Christy Henrich's case thrusts this reality right in our faces, so to speak. And we need that—some of us more desperately than others. Left unchallenged, the lies that fuel magical thinking, illusions of control and shame will surely steal our joy, if not our lives.

LIES, SHAME, AND THE ILLUSION OF PERFECTION

One of the things I love about the Gospel is that it is so democratic. It says we're *all* a mess! I'm neither more of a mess than you, nor you more of a mess than me in God's eyes. That's true whether you or I ever believe it. And what a tragedy that so many of us never do.

In contrast to the democracy of the Gospel, shame is the soul-deep belief that something is horribly and uniquely wrong with me that is not wrong with anybody else in the entire world. If I am bound by shame, I feel *literally* worth *less* than other people.

Where did we ever get this blatantly unbiblical concept of shame? Somebody lied to us when we were too young to read and understand the Bible for ourselves or to accurately interpret the world around us. Actually, it was probably a whole lot of somebodies who likely believed the lie themselves. (As we're learning, lies of conviction, taught by deceived deceivers, are no less destructive than deception perpetrated with cunning and malice.)

> The lie creating and perpetuating shame teaches that human beings should have no flaws, problems, or needs. In other words, people ought to be perfect. The implication is: people can be perfect if they really try their hardest.

Believing this lie of perfection produces a shame-based lifestyle marked by many characteristics ranging from joy-sapping to downright self-destruction.

RECOGNIZING SYMPTOMS OF SHAME

Many of us have lived with shame so long we're oblivious to it. Here are some of the physical, cognitive, and relational signs of shame that can help us recognize its effects in our lives.

Physical Signs of Shame

Many of the physical conditions associated with embarassment or humiliation occur in the presence of shame. They can include:

- *Increased body temperature* (a warm flush or even a "hot flash"),
- *Nausea,*
- *Heaviness in the chest* (perhaps even to the point of feeling panicky),
- *Poor eye-contact and hesitant speech patterns,*
- *Body-minimizing posture,* as if trying to be invisible or use very little space.

Cognitive Signs of Shame

Thinking patterns shaped by shame contain most, if not all, of the following features.

- *Demeaning self-labeling.* I say to myself, "I'm such an idiot, bad person, rotten Christian," etc.
- *Guilt-proneness.* I see myself as the cause of any difficulty or disturbance within any relational group such as family, church, etc.
- *Compulsive rationalization.* I feel compelled to explain/excuse oneself to deflect criticism and "save face."
- *Personalization.* I perceive every experience as a commentary on my identity and worth.
- *All-or-nothing thinking.* On a continuum of one to ten, there are only two possibilities. One. Or ten!

Relational Signs of Shame

We'll look more closely at relationships in chapter 8, but here are a few traits common to shame-bound relationships. They all reflect the fact that we will feel ineligible for mutually respectful relationships if we believe that we are worth *less* than others.

- *Rescuing,* also known as "needing to be needed." Doubting that any healthy person would freely *choose* to relate to us, we have to find ways to be of service so people will *need* to relate to us. (We may even become professional "people helpers" to insure this!)

- *Tolerating disrespect and even abuse.* We often live as if disrespectful and even dangerous relationships are better than no relationships at all.
- *Trust problems* created by childhood betrayals of trust. This applies to God too.
- *Hypersensitivity to rejection based on fear of abandonment.* We will be deeply hurt, feel panicky or even end a relationship if someone forgets a lunch date, etc.
- *Approval-addiction.* We will sacrifice personal standards, work past the point of exhaustion, etc. because we crave approval from significant people in our lives.
- *Fear of criticism and anger* because it means withdrawal of approval.

Did you recognize yourself in a cluster of these traits? If so, you will probably also recognize that your sense of shame gets triggered in some situations far more than in others. These are some of the typical experiences that elicit shame-laden feelings and thoughts.

- *Being late* to important events.
- *Forgetting* names or information, especially in the presence of others.
- *Making factual mistakes or judgement errors*, especially if observed by others.
- *Failing to achieve a stated goal* such as getting a desired job or date with certain person, lose specific number of pounds, etc.
- *Disappointing others' expectations*

Obviously, this list of shame-inducing experiences is representative, not exhaustive. Obviously, too, all these situations share a common characteristic: they reveal personal imperfections.

PERFECTIONISM:
THE MAGICAL SHAME-SHIELD

You will recall that in chapter 2 we noted that consistently adequate parents in healthy families expect human imperfections and understand something about child development. As a result these imperfect but well-functioning parents usually have pretty realistic expectations for their children. And in turn, their children are likely to adopt pretty realistic expectations for themselves and *their* children.

In contrast, life-shackling perfectionism becomes the defense of choice for those of us tutored in unrealistic expectation in childhood. And if we've been raised with *unrealistic* expectations, we might not even recognize a *realistic* one if it bit us on the nose! Here are two examples of the unrealistic expectations typically conveyed by parents' comments to kids (of all ages) in unhealthy families. I'll couple each with a more realistic alternative.

Unrealistic Expectation (spoken to a seventh grader with a mediocre report card): "There's no excuse for someone with your IQ not getting all *A*s."

Realistic Expectation "Your mom/dad and I know you are bright enough to do better. We'd like to see you improve your study habits and your grades."

Unrealistic Expectation (spoken to a recent college graduate with a new job): "With all we've spent on your education, you'll get a big promotion and raise in no time."

Realistic Expectation "We sure think you are well-qualified to do a great job for that company."

Which statement in each pair sounded more familiar? Could you identify the control-fantasy in each unrealistic expectation? Being intelligent and having a college education certainly contribute to receiving top grades and promotions. But the opinions of teachers and bosses and the abilities of other students and employees also impact those outcomes. Or, to use magical-thinking terminology, intelligence and college education strongly *influence* grades and promotions, but they do not *control* them, since grades and promotions involve the wills and skills of other people.

By the way, in many shame-based families, unrealistic expectation messages contain powerful emotional "zingers" such as, "This family expects winners, not losers." Or as one person I know learned from his parents: "Second place is no place!"

Those comments offer a clue to the two most prevalent shame-perpetuating lies that tether us to an unbiblical self-concept and envelop us in perfectionism, which we use to shield ourselves from the painful feelings shame elicits. These lies are:

(1) I must do everything perfectly.

(2) My personal worth depends on how much and how well I achieve.

When we recall that youngsters believe their parents know the truth about everything and always tell the truth, we can understand how parental expectations and treatment of their children become identity statements imprinted in the wet cement of young minds. Believing those lies makes even more sense when we recognize that parents' unrealistic and perfectionistic expectations are nearly always accompanied by performance-based expressions of approval, relabeled as love. Thus, *doing* more and better equates to *being* more and better.

When those lies and their logical conclusions interact with the all-or-nothing thinking so prevalent in poorly-functioning families, perfectionism abounds. All-or-nothing thinking offers only two extreme possibilities in any situation. So when it comes to evaluating ourselves, we are either perfect or we're garbage! Few of us want to think of ourselves as garbage, so that only leaves one alternative. We must be perfect. And how will we know we're perfect and not garbage? We must do everything perfectly.

As we've discovered, perfectionism flourishes in the soil of unrealistic expectation and all-or-nothing thinking. But it comes to fullest bloom when fed by our fantasy-driven compulsion to control.

SHAME, PERFECTIONISM, AND CONTROL FANTASIES

Earlier in this chapter, we identified the lie that creates and perpetuates shame, namely, human beings should have no flaws, problems, or needs. In other words, people ought to be perfect. And we saw the implications contained in that lie:

(1) I can be perfect if I really try my hardest.

(2) If I'm not perfect, then I am disgustingly different, essentially sub-human, and therefore worth *less* than other people.

The *second* implication captures what I am calling a sense of unbiblical shame. And implication number one becomes our shield against the painful feelings generated by implication number two.

As long as we believe the lie that flaws, imperfections, mistakes, poor judgment, and other "goofs" mark us as sub-human, we will be satisfied with nothing less than perfection. Or at least, perfection's kissing-cousin, "being the very best"—which brings us back to our gymnast Christy Henrich.

Less than a year before her death, Christy's coach pressured her into beginning therapy with an eating disorders specialist. In an attempt to spotlight the problem, and with the Henrich family's consent, the therapist revealed customarily confidential information from her four months of work with Christy.

> [Christy] felt shame toward everything in her life and it drove her obsessive-compulsive behavior, her perfectionism, her self-punishment. . . . She was afraid of failure. She was terrified of being fat. [Remember, Christy believed she didn't win because she wasn't thin enough.] No matter how well she did, the message she gave herself was that it wasn't enough, it wasn't OK.[2]

The therapist also described the agony Christy felt for missing the 1988 Olympic team by .118 of a point. Christy believed she had failed her family who sacrificed so much for her, her coach, and the younger athletes who looked up to her at the gymnastics club.

Can you recognize the threads of shame and magical thinking woven through Christy Henrich's belief system? (Remember, we *live* what we believe.) Christy believed that if she wasn't the best, she was a failure. She also believed that her—as she perceived it—excess weight prevented her from being the best. So if she could just get thin enough, she would be able to control the outcome of the gymnastic competitions. She could finally be perfect enough to be judged "the best."

But there was more. She did not just fail to make the Olympic team, which would be painfully disappointing for any world-class athlete. Christy believed "she *was* a failure." In other words, her success as a performer translated into her worth as a person. Statements by Christy's fiancé before her death corroborate this view of Christy's performance-based self-concept.

The young man said she was "morose about her prospects after gymnastics. *It was who she was.* She spent eight hours a day for twelve years trying to be the best and now it was about to end."[3] (Emphasis added.)

It's almost as if the end of Christy's opporunities to be the best at gymnastics spelled the end of her very personhood. That perspective makes sense if someone operates by magical-thinking's control illusions. And anytime we buy into the concept of performance-based worth, we're trafficking in illusions of control.

The fantasy says if I improve my performance, I increase my worth. So, as long as I have another chance to *perform* perfectly, I can cling to the dream that someday I'll finally *be* perfect. Obviously, that mindset keeps me in control. And it keeps me from accepting the disturbing reality that even when I've performed *my* very best, those evaluating it may not think my efforts are *the* very best. That judgment depends upon the judges' value systems as well as my ability and determination. Certainly that's the case in sports like gymnastics, ice skating, and diving.

How sadly ironic that the eating disorder Henrich used to serve her control-oriented goal of weight reduction eventually commanded more and more control over her life. In time, her servant became her master. And that produced a terminal sense of shame Christy Henrich never overcame.

Christy's therapist said that Henrich felt agonizing shame about having an eating disorder that hospitalized her repeatedly. After all, her nickname was E.T. — short for Extra Tough. Everyone who knew Christy came away impressed with her extraordinary determination to reach her goal of being the best. Yet she couldn't seem to conquer the problem that was sapping her energy and reducing her to a skeleton.

I have two articles about Christy written eleven months apart. In the first, I learned that about eight months before Christy's death several Olympic gymnasts performed at a benefit to raise money to help pay her huge medical bills. The author added these comments at the end:

> Christy Henrich, who while hospitalized sees her family on weekends, appeared at the benefit briefly. She may be released in the fall, but her therapy will continue for years.[4]

The later article sounds a heartbreaking postlude to the first. It quotes her gymnastics coach, Al Fong, who originally confronted his star pupil and contacted a therapist and nutritionist for her. He also told Christy's parents about his concerns that she had an eating disorder. Fong said, "The Henrichs were shocked. . . . They also were fiercely resistant." In fact it seems that her parents experienced some degree of shame about having a child with an eating disorder. When Christy's mother contacted a U.S.A. Gymnastics official to ask for financial help, she spoke of her daughter's multiple hospitalizations for a "disease." But she never named the disease.

Neither Christy nor her parents stayed in counseling with the specialist her coach contacted. Fong said, "She hated it. Abolutely hated it." And as long as Christy refused help, Fong barred her from his gym.

After the 1992 Barcelona Olympics, Henrich told Fong she was "really jazzed" and wanted to train for the 1996 Olympics. She said, "I know I can do it." Again, the coach told her she would have to resolve her eating disorder. Christy never contacted him again. And neither she nor her parents ever sought help.

Seven months before she died, Christy told a friend she ate no more than an apple a day, sometimes only a slice. Two months before her death, a reporter phoned Henrich to ask her how she was doing. Christy said she wanted to get back into shape but wouldn't return to therapy. *"She was going to do it on her own."*[5]

That's it. That's the heart-cry of all control illusions: *I don't need any help, I can do it on my own.* Christy Henrich never surrendered the illusion that she could control the life-threatening disorder of which she was so ashamed. Yet neither Christy's determination nor her family's denial could stop the deadly progression of truth about eating disorders. And in the end, truth won. It always does.

How tragic, you may be thinking. You also may think that Christy Henrich's story bears little resemblance to yours since you don't aspire to such lofty goals as a berth on the Olympic team. Perhaps you are what I call a discouraged perfectionist.

THE OPPOSITE EXTREME: DISCOURAGED PERFECTIONISTS

Since they insist on aiming at a humanly unreachable target, perfectionists live constantly with varying degrees of disappointment with themselves. Sometimes, weary and despondent perfectionists swing to the opposite extreme of not trying at all to study, eat right, clean house, keep business records up to date, have personal devotions, etc.

Trudy knows about that only too well.

When I met Trudy, a Christian in her mid-thirties, she was fifty pounds overweight and deeply discouraged about life in general. And herself in particular. Trudy's well-educated, high-energy parents expected a lot from their firstborn daughter right from the start. As she explained, "I just always seemed to be out of synch with my folks and their plans for me. I mean, I didn't deliberately try to disappoint them. It just seemed to come naturally. No matter what I did, I always heard, 'if you'd try harder' or 'we had so hoped you'd do whatever.' Eventually I realized I would never measure up. I think I just got tired of trying."

Trudy seemed paralyzed by shame about nearly every aspect of herself, including her obesity, her singleness, her job as secretary, and her nonexistent prayer life. After all, she was taught that, by her age, she should be a slim, successful, wife, mother, and spiritual giant.

Trudy began attending a ten-week Christian "recovery from shame" support group. Four weeks into it, she declared, "I recognize lots of shame stuff in my life, but I can't figure out where it came from. I mean, my folks never neglected or abused me. And I sure don't remember them telling me I was 'uniquely flawed and worth less than others' if I wasn't perfect. [Trudy was quoting the definition of shame in the book the group was reading.] Gosh no, they always encouraged me to be the very best at everything I did."

By now, you're sophisticated enough at spotting shame-inducing lies to catch that one, aren't you? So were many members of Trudy's support group. And eventually, Trudy learned to recognize the "lie of conviction" undergirding the expectation to be "the very best at everything." She also came to to see her parents as the loving but shame-bound people they are.

Now, if you're like me, you're probably hoping to read that Trudy lost fifty pounds, married a wonderful guy, and recently completed her masters in counseling so she could help others overcome the effects of magical thinking and shame. Actually, Trudy has lost some, but not all, of her excess weight. She's still single and still a secretary. But she would tell you that she is learning to believe that her weight, marital status, and occupation do not define her. She is also learning that an inconsistent prayer life is better than none at all. Most important, Trudy has finally begun to believe she is who *God* says she is.

SEEING OURSELVES
AS GOD SEES US[6]

In James 1:23-25, God says that, like a clear mirror, the *Bible* reflects our true identity. And God promises He will bless us when we live based on what we learn about ourselves from His Word rather than casually glancing at it and then forgetting what we see.

Evangelical churches and leaders traditionally teach that we are unworthy of God's gift of grace. They're right of course. Grace is a gift precisely because we cannot be good enough to earn it. However, some of these churches and leaders also teach that we are worthless. Not true, according to God.

Have you ever stopped to consider that an object's value is established by its purchase price? In fact, *every buyer subjectively attributes worth to his or her purchases.* And the purchase price clearly reveals the buyer's personal opinion regarding the value of that purchase.

For some incomprehensibly gracious reason, and despite the fact that we are all hopelessly marred by sin, God chooses to make us His adopted heirs and kingdom priests. And what is the purchase price God paid to accomplish His goal? "The precious blood of Christ," according to 1 Peter 1:19. Yes! I know it sounds impossibly grandiose to say it this way, but by the price He paid, God openly established our worth. For when it came to our purchase price, God was more concerned about what He "saved" than what He spent.

Are we unworthy? *Absolutely.* Are we worthless? Absolutely *not!* This baffling blend of truths creates an unfathomable paradox for us. And hardcore all-or-nothing thinkers find this especially troublesome.

I don't think paradoxes, two apparently contradictory truths existing together, bother God at all. What's more, this unworthy-but-not-worthless paradox suggests other paradoxical aspects of human personhood, such as our great potential and firm limitations, our capacities for unblinking cruelty and selfless compassion, and many more.

God sees us perfectly and describes us precisely in Scripture. So, learning to see ourselves as God sees us requires looking into our perfect mirror, the *Bible.* But it also demands the surrender of some control fantasies we may have been depending on to feel safe.

As long as we believe and live the lie that our intrinsic worth comes from the quality of our accomplishments, we retain control. Of course, it's really just an *illusion* of control. But clinging to that illusion keeps some of us feeling safe. As we saw through Christy Henrich's extreme example, that illusion of control, with its imaginary sense of safety, is actually anything but safe.

Here we are again at one of those important choice points in life. Do we keep trying to *do* more and better so we will *be* more and better? Or will we receive the gift of intrinsic, unalterable worth attributed to and bestowed on us by God, apart from our doing and beyond our control?

THE LIFE-CHANGING CHOICE: WHOSE EYES?

I've been told that a circus trainer will tie a baby elephant to a stake in the ground to make it manageable. Naturally the animal tugs with all its strength to get away, but soon learns it can't. Eventually, elephants stop tugging, so that even when fully grown and strong enough to break away, they no longer try.

In a sense, many of us are still shackled to the distorted self-concepts we learned in childhood. Like those circus elephants, we haven't exercised our increased powers of choice to break free. Yes, I know it's a lot more complicated than the elephant story suggests. We humans have to contend with our control-lusting hearts, deeply-ingrained parental identity messages, "perks" — such as prestige and popularity — that come from performance-focused living, and much more.

Despite all the forces tethering us to magical-thinking and shame, the God of truth calls us to look into His Word to see ourselves realistically. Essentially, God asks us to turn from searching other human beings' eyes for evidence of our worth. He bids us to look into *His* eyes instead.

Over my years as a counselor, I've had the privilege of working with many remarkable Christian adults raised in remarkably hurtful families. That group includes Paula, the thirtysomething middle child of alcoholic parents. By God's grace and lots of hard work, Paula and her husband had created a loving, Christ-centered home for their two sons. Nevertheless, Paula continued to struggle with a distorted, denigrating self-concept.

You'll recall that God uses a multitude of amazingly creative ways to teach us about His character as well as about our identity in

His eyes. Paula certainly discovered that. You see, she and her husband lived on several acres that included a few sheep. During the time Paula was in counseling, her ewe totally rejected one of its newborn lambs. God used this situation to help Paula experience personally, not just believe intellectually, the truth of Psalm 27:10. That verse says: "When my father and mother forsake me, then the LORD will take me up" (KJV).

Here's a portion of a note Paula wrote me. (The italicized words were underlined in her note.)

> I've enclosed a photo of my orphan lamb, that the Lord has taught me *so* much through. Now I need to *apply* what I've learned to my own life! She didn't turn out with all the beautiful markings the others have, but in my eyes, she's just as beautiful. (Boy, do I need to learn from that!)

Paula easily identified with that less-than-beautiful lamb who had been orphaned by her mother's utter rejection. Paula recognized also that she loved that forsaken little lamb even though it could do nothing to earn her love. In fact, it cost her a lot in extra work. Surely, Paula concluded, *God* was more merciful and loving than *she*. As she cuddled and hand-fed that orphan lamb, Paula began to experience the reality of being held, nurtured, and adopted by her Heavenly Parent.

Paula said that she needed to learn from the fact that the orphaned lamb was beautiful in her shepherdess' eyes even though it was found unacceptable in its parent's eyes. Don't we all need to learn from that to some degree?

I phoned Paula a few days ago to obtain permission to use her note. She told me that she continues to work hard to make real in her heart and life what she learned from her orphaned lamb.

Whose eyes will we trust to see our true identity most realistically? Some hypercritical, never-fully-satisfied shamer's eyes? Our own illusion-clouded eyes? Or our gracious, Good Shepherd's eyes? The choice is ours.

Think about It

What do you look to as the basis of your personal worth? (HINT: since we live what we believe, examine your *life*, e.g., schedule, emotional highs and lows, etc., for the answer.)

Are you willing to relinquish your illusion of control regarding *being* more by *doing* more? If not, why not?

If you are willing to relinquish that illusion, here are some Bible verses that will help you begin seeing yourself as God sees you.

1. *John 1:12; 1 Peter 2:9* (I am a child of God and I belong to Him.)
2. *Romans 8:35-39* (Nothing can separate me from God's love.)
3. *Ephesians 1:4* (I am chosen by God.)
4. *Ephesians 2:18; 3:12* (I have access to God through Jesus.)
5. *Colossians 2:13-14* (I am forgiven and my sin-debt is paid.)
6. *Romans 8:1* (I am not condemned.)
7. *Romans 5:1* (I have peace with God through my Lord Jesus Christ.)
8. *Colossians 1:13* (I have been rescued from the dominion of darkness and brought into the kingdom of God's Son.)

If you're journaling, you may want to write each verse in your own words along with a personal application. Remember, these verses and *many* others tell you who you really are in your Creator's eyes. Here's a hypothetical example of such an entry.

Colossians 2:13-14. I am forgiven of all my sins because Jesus paid the purchase price for me.

> I don't need to continue punishing myself for my sexual promiscuity in high school. God knows my heart so He knows I have sincerely repented. That sin does not make me ineligible for God's gracious blessings.

Pray about It

DEAR LORD, Please help me believe Your message about my true identity as I study Your Word. Thank You so much for adopting me into Your family. I know I can't do anything to earn this, but I want to live more consistently in a way that reflects my relationship as Your child. Please teach me how to do that. AMEN.

Learn More about It

Illusions of control can distort virtually every aspect of our lives. Nowhere do we see that more clearly than in the realm of emotions. That's what we investigate next.

SEVEN

Illusions of Control
in Managing Our Emotions

Did you hear about the cowboy and Indian riding across the desert toward town? The hungry cowboy kept talking about food. "When I get into town, I'm going to get the biggest, thickest steak I can find and really chow down," he announced. The Indian was silent. Finally, the cowboy said, "We haven't eaten all day, aren't you hungry?" The Indian said he wasn't.

When they finally got to town and ordered their meals, the Indian ate twice as much as his companion. The baffled cowboy said, "Out on the desert you said you weren't hungry, what's going on?" The Indian responded, "Not wise to be hungry when no food."

As an adult, the insightful Indian in our story intentionally chose to play a mind game to control his hunger. In remarkably similar ways, many of us as children had to play mind games to manage our emotions. The more emotionally impoverished our birth families, the more we needed powerful means to deaden our emotions. Magical-thinking's control fantasies were just the ticket!

At this point in our lives, we may feel like the little boy whose parents repeatedly forced him to sit down when he wanted to stand up in his chair. After finally giving in, he angrily announced, "I may be sitting on the outside, but I'm standing on the inside!" In a sense, many of us learned that we had to "sit on" our confusion, anger, fear, sadness, longing for tender touch and genuine acceptance, and so much more.

Those sat-on parts of our emotional natures may now be, in effect, jumping up and down, screaming frantically, "My turn! My turn!" As a result, we can sometimes have the vague sensation that something within us is trying to get our attention. Something we don't want to acknowledge.

For instance, have you ever experienced or expressed some strong emotion that seemed alien to you? Maybe you said something like, "What got into me?" Perhaps the more realistic question would be, "What got *out* of me?" Of course, whether or not we typically try to "sit on" (read that: control out of existence) our emotions reflect what we have been taught to believe about emotions.

IDENTIFYING OUR BELIEFS ABOUT EMOTIONS

As with every other area of our lives, our beliefs about emotions probably contain a mixture of illusion and reality, also known as lies and truths. For example, we may have learned to believe that emotions are unspiritual and immature—really quite embarrassing for Christian adults. As a result, we might put a lot of energy into eliminating them. In reality, our emotions are a divinely designed part of our human nature which reflects God's image. What's more, Jesus came to take away our *sins,* not our *feelings!*

Some people have been taught to believe that it is actually dangerous for them to have strong feelings. They fear their emotions will make them "fall apart," "go crazy," or even harm someone. The truth is that emotions are neither good nor bad. And adults can learn to express their feelings appropriately, even when they didn't learn that as children.

LEARNING THE RULES ABOUT FEELINGS

Nearly every book or article about dysfunctional families discusses the so-called rules children learn growing up in them. These rules always include some variation of "don't feel."

Perhaps, it's more realistic to say that most unhealthy families have radically different rules for adults than for children when it comes to displaying feelings. It's not unusual for one parent to be the designated anger-carrier. Often it's the father—especially in Christian families. Mother may be assigned the task of expressing sadness and anxiety for the family.

The children usually are taught that they should feel only emotions such as happiness and gratitude. After all, what other feelings would you expect children to have in perfect, problem-free families? Clearly, all unpleasant emotions like anger and sadness must be off-limits to children in these shame-based, perfection-posturing, emotionally overcontrolling homes. Now you may be wondering what happens when *parents* express these emotions. You probably won't be too surprised to learn that they're apt to be denied or disguised, often by blaming the *children* for causing them.

Children learn which feelings are on the family's short list of approved emotions from their parents' spoken and unspoken messages. Let's look at examples of illusional and truthful rule-implying messages regarding anger, which is a typically unacceptable emotion for children in families that seek to create the illusion of perfection.

Illusional Message(s): "You shouldn't get angry." (Or: "You shouldn't feel that way." Or, in overcontrolling *religious* families: "God doesn't want you to get angry." Or, still worse: "God doesn't like little boys and girls who get angry.")

Implicit Rule(s): I am bad if I feel angry. (Add this spiritually abusive possibility: God won't love me if I feel angry.)

Truthful Message: "I can see that you're angry, but in this family we don't allow hitting. You can learn to be angry without hitting. Let's talk about how."

Implicit Rule: I am not supposed to hit people when I'm angry.

Which message and rule more clearly reflects the biblical view of anger expressed in Ephesians 4:26? That verse says: "*Be angry, and yet do not sin.*" Living in a sinful world, we are indulging in illusions to think that we would never feel angry. Or *should* never feel angry.

Why wouldn't, for example, malicious deception, injustice, authority abuse, or oppression of the less powerful anger us? Those things anger God, according to Scripture. And if it is *right* to be angry about what angers God where *others* are concerned, why is it *wrong* to be angry about what angers God where *we* are concerned?

That double standard only makes sense in families where adults want to be able to deceive unjustly and abuse their authority and power without having to face their children's appropriate anger. In such shame-bound, illusion-laden families, children invariably learn that being the perfect person they're expected to be includes displaying the *"take-everything-without-feeling-anything factor."* This highly valued trait demands and cultivates the capacity to endure any circumstance whatsoever without feeling anything but "fine" and without behaving any way except "nice."

The more unhealthy and shame-bound the family, the more important it is to appearance-preserving parents to tutor their children in this phony feelings curriculum. Think about the Catch-22 kind of crazymaking this creates as unstable, troubled families *elicit* strong, distressing emotions in children, while simultaneously forbidding children to *feel* those emotions!

We might not be shocked to discover these emotion-flattening messages and expectations among our heathen neighbors. But how do we explain this phenomenon among conservative, church-going folks? Maybe part of the problem is *where* they're going to church.

WHEN CHURCHES SUPPORT ILLUSIONS ABOUT EMOTIONS

Perhaps you've discovered that some churches have expectations and rules about emotions that are disquietingly similar to those taught children in dysfunctional families. Sadly, many of these feeling-phobic churches proudly proclaim they are "Bible-believing." However, they seem to be pretty selective about which parts of the Bible they believe.

The Bible does not depict emotions as some troublesome childhood condition we should outgrow. Disowning our authentic feelings doesn't make us more mature. It makes us less the beings God made us to be.

God created human beings with the capacity to experience a full range of emotions, pleasant and unpleasant. We see portions of this broad emotional panorama displayed in Eccclesiastes 3:4 as the verse speaks of times to weep, laugh, mourn, and dance. And this concept certainly does not appear in the Old Testament only.

In Romans 12:15, we're told to rejoice with the rejoicing and weep with the weeping. In fact, it makes a lot of sense to me that living on this sin-polluted planet would likely produce at least as much weeping as rejoicing. Maybe more. Yet many Christians are taught to feel like spiritually immature crybabies unless they can skip and giggle their way through even the most anguish-ridden situations while feeling "fine" and being "nice."

In fact, I've begun to suspect that some evangelicals value being *nice* more than being *real*. Perhaps they think nice is included in the "fruit of the Spirit" listed in Galatians, chapter 5! But it's not. In fact, when we look into the Gospels, we quickly discover that *Jesus was not always nice*. And He certainly didn't feel *fine* all the time. Check for yourself.

And while we're on this subject, I might as well confess. Even though I rejoice that my sins have been rolled away, I am not necessarily happy all the day! Where did we come up with unbiblical, reality-defying ideas like that?

Jesus is the supreme realist. And He certainly never deceived His followers with the illusional promise of all-the-day happiness. Instead, He promised something far more wonderful: the eternal joy of His presence, unrelated to the happenings of our days.

Unceasingly, Jesus called people out of illusional living and into truth. He still does. I conclude from this that if we base our lives on the belief that Christians are supposed to be hap-hap-happy all the day, we're going to feel called to *Fake It for Jesus' Sake*. And if so, we aren't listening to our Savior or really looking at His example. Lots of other folks may call us to the phony feelings lifestyle. Jesus never will.

As many of us can testify who came from families and churches who overcontrolled emotions, shaming ourselves for experiencing distressing emotions only intensifies them. More than once, I've been depressed about my depression. Ever been angry at yourself for not being able to control your anger out of existence, even though you've been taught that "good Christians never get angry"?

This business of how we experience and express our emotions brings us back to the unavoidable issue of control. Most of the Christians I know specialize in the overcontrolling extreme. This overcontrolling style involves strenuous efforts designed to block all awareness of feelings we've been taught to believe we "shouldn't" have. And most of the time we overcontrolling, emotion-blockers don't even recognize what we're doing.

We also may not realize what this overcontrolling of emotions does to us.

EMOTIONAL ILLUSION AND
PHYSICAL REALITY

Instead of attempting to pull rabbits from apparently empty hats, some of us overcontrollers are, in effect, trying to make our distressing-emotions "hat" appear empty when it's full of embarassing bunnies! And sometimes our magic trick may feel more like trying to keep tigers in a tank. There's one, not-so-small problem with this disappearing trick: our bodies aren't being fooled.

Feelings are real and feelings have a history. Unpleasant feelings, such as anger, fear, and sadness, are present to tell us that something in our lives needs tending.

If we don't tend promptly and appropriately to these strong, distressing emotions, we may end up tending to lots of other distressing things — potentially life-threatening physical problems, for instance.

Over the past few decades, many studies have demonstrated a strong connection between emotional and physical well-being. Most of these findings suggest that the primary source of trouble isn't strong emotions themselves as much as our attempts to block them from our awareness.

For instance, in one study, researchers divided subjects into three groups on the basis of psychological assessments and an early-memory test that looked for signs of emotional distress. Then the subjects participated in stressful tasks that included making-up stories about ambiguous drawings designed to raise themes that some people find psychologically threatening. Subjects' stress reactions were measured by unusual jumps in heart rate and blood pressure.

Researchers concluded that people with hidden distress (group one) were twice as reactive to stress as genuinely healthy people (group two). And the hidden stress subjects were even more reactive than people who acknowledged they were distressed (group three). A second study confirmed these results.

The primary researcher summed up the studies by saying, "We

know that being emotionally distressed, being constantly anxious or constantly depressed isn't so healthy, but the new work suggests that suppressing distress may be even worse.[1]

Echoing this conclusion, even more recent research revealed that, people who *"usually suppress anger"* metabolize fats more slowly than others, which may be a key reason hostility and heart attacks are linked.[2]

Trying to live in the fantasyland of "forever fine" negatively affects more than just our cardiovascular functioning, especially if we have been sitting on genuinely awful past experiences and the feelings they elicit.

Trauma-induced emotions don't disappear magically. Instead, studies of sexually abused women suggest that the unspoken emotional anguish gets translated into physical and behavioral cries of pain. After an extensive review of medical studies, researchers at Stanford University School of Medicine found that sexual abuse has been linked to numerous health problems in women. For instance, some studies showed that "as many as two-thirds of women with chronic pelvic pain had a history of incest and molestation." Other studies documented a correlation between sexual abuse and obesity, other eating disorders, smoking, drinking, and other body-bashing behaviors.[3]

From what we've learned about the dynamics in severely troubled families, we know that the children aren't allowed to talk truthfully about their abuse or reveal the normal, human emotions that accompany such treatment. The Stanford research validates what many of us have discovered already: our bodies often express the painful realities our minds try to totally deny.

Doesn't it make sense that the God of truth would create us to function with greatest total well-being when we live in truth? I believe this reveals another facet of the incomprehensibly rich reality of being bearers of our Creator's image. But I think God is up to something more, as well.

I find Ecclesiastes 3:15 one of the most fascinating verses in the Bible. Here it is in both an ancient and a modern translation.

> That which hath been is now; and that which is to be hath already been; and God requireth that which is past (KJV).
> That which is has been already, and that which will be has already been, for God seeks what has passed by (NASB).

It's that last phrase that captures my interest particularly. A former pastor once told me that the words "what has passed by," are better understood as "what has been driven away." In other words, we drive away God's lessons, so He repeats them.

Said differently, God keeps bringing back the rejected reality we push away until we deal with the hidden pain that He knows needs to be healed. He created our bodies with the capacity to serve that end. God desires to give the hidden-parts wisdom we need to change emotion-numbing beliefs and behaviors because He knows they harm us far more than dealing honestly with distressing feelings ever could.

So don't despise your body for using physical symptoms to reveal the emotional pain you've been pretending isn't there. Pain has been called the gift nobody wants. Yet if the Giver is good, the ultimate purpose of all His gifts will also be good. But a whole lot of us may not be ready to face that reality just now. We want to hold on to the magical emotion-blocking mechanisms that have become so comfortingly familiar.

We haven't yet noticed, perhaps, that what we're holding on to is also holding on to us.

"MAGICAL" EMOTION BLOCKERS

Remember those folks who habitually suppressed their feelings of anger in one of the studies we discussed earlier? I'm worried about them. As slow fat metabolizers, they are in big trouble if, like me, the only emotion management skill they learned in childhood was *eating*. And considering the profits racked up by the weight-loss industry, I doubt that I am the only person about whom this is true. How about you? What do you use to control away feelings you don't want to face?

We can use food (too much or too little), sexual arousal, exercise, relationships, and/or all the "isms," e.g., alcoholism, workaholism, etc., to numb emotions we believe we shouldn't experience. If I'm right about all these substances and activities functioning as emotion-blockers, we would expect to see what is usually called "addictive behavior" in people who come from those unhealthy homes that both elicit and forbid distressing feelings.

In an article titled "Abused Children, Addicted Adults," Dr. Patrick Carnes presents evidence supporting that exact connection. In a four-year study of over 1,000 recovering "sex addicts," Dr. Carnes and his colleagues concluded that all addictions were, in part, solutions to the traumas and stresses of child abuse. Of the more than 1,000 subjects, 81 percent had been sexually abused; 72 percent were physically abused; and 97 percent were emotionally abused. Further, they found that *"the more severely participants were abused sexually and physically, the more addictions they developed."*[4]

Still other recent research found that nearly nine in ten alcoholic women suffered physical or sexual abuse as girls. This study of almost 500 women adds to the evidence connecting childhood abuse to adults' life-dominating problems such as alcoholism.[5]

I realize that many Christians respond to statements like that by rolling their eyes in disgust at what they see as just another attempt to help adults avoid responsibility for their sinful choices. No doubt, many people will use these findings to do just that. However, I'd like to suggest we view this research as another indication that early childhood experiences profoundly shape our choices, even those we don't realize we've made. One of these choices might be using whatever emotional anesthetic necessary to avoid feeling as overwhelmingly terrified and out-of-control as we felt when we were helpless children.

Now all emotion-blocking substances and activities, whether legal or illegal, share one annoying trait. They wear off. So as we continue to self-medicate our distress and pain, we must gradually increase the dose to get the desired numbness. Before long we can find ourselves organizing our daily lives around this magical emotion-blocking. If we miss a dose, frightening, confusing emotions begin to stir again. So then, of course, we need to spend even more energy pursuing the longed-for fantasy of "forever feeling fine."

Those of us who have traveled this yellow-brick road of illusion know only too well that life can quickly resemble a roller coaster that looks something like Figure 7-1 on page 105.

Notice that the number five reality on our roller coaster ride is a bit lower than the number one reality. That's because whenever we persist in pursuing magical thinking's illusions of control, we create more—not less—confusion and pain for ourselves. And often for others too.

As always, truth makes us free even though it may first make us miserable. And unless we're willing to face the real, distressing emo-

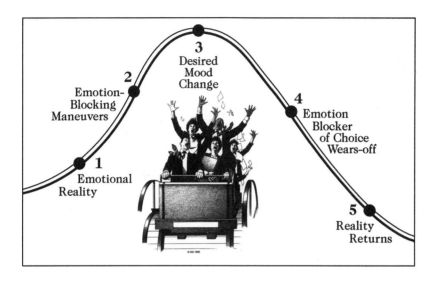

Figure 7-1

tions connected to our yesterdays, we're not likely to pull free from the phony-feelings roller coaster ride we're on today.

We've spent most of this chapter examining how overcontrolling emotions translate into efforts to block any awareness of feelings we believe we "shouldn't" have. On the other hand, *under*controlling emotions leads us to the grown-down emotional instability of young children.

UNDERCONTROLLING ILLUSIONS

Grown-down undercontrollers seem to insist on living the magical-thinking illusion that everything and everyone must revolve around their desires. This infantile approach buys a one-way, nonstop ticket to the fantasyland roller coaster.

In Fantasyland, there are never any flat tires, people with twenty items in their grocery cart standing ahead of us in the "twelve-items-or-less" line, unfriendly neighbors, fallen soufflés, cancelled flights, you name it. Unfortunately, we don't live in that illusional zipcode.

Here in Reality City, all those unpleasant experiences, or others like them and far worse, occur with distressing regularity. And they all have two qualities in common. First, we can't control them.

(That's the part we really hate!) Second, they confront us with a choice about how to respond.

Let's take the flat tire situation for example. If I believe I am supposed to be living in Fantasyland where I can control everything according to my desires, I'm likely to become awfully upset when my tire goes flat. Especially if I'm driving somewhere important that includes a fixed starting time. I may get so angry, I kick the tire hard enough to injure my toe. This, of course, adds medical bills and pain to the incovenience of my flat tire. And I might believe my anger is so justified, I not only hold on to it for a while, but I also freely dump it on anyone unfortunate enough to cross my path.

On the other hand, I could choose to change the tire (or get someone else to do it) and continue my drive with only mild annoyance at the delay.

As adults, we have the cognitive development necessary to do what we could not do as children. We can learn to step back from an emotionally distressing situation and ask ourselves some questions that will lead to more realistic and appropriate emotional control. We ask questions like these:

- Does my perception of the situation match the reality of the situation?
- Am I taking this too personally?
- Am I trying to control who and what I can only influence?

Answering these and similar questions will help us grow up and out of the magical kingdoms we so often construct to enthrone ourselves with the divine right to rule with our wishes.

CHOOSING EMOTIONAL REALITY

Even if you couldn't relate to the emotional-overcontrolling most abuse survivors practice, you may have recognized yourself in the example of emotional-undercontrolling. In contrast to those two unhealthy, unbiblical extremes, we can learn to exercise *appropriate* control over the expression of our authentic emotions.

We're standing at another choice point, aren't we? It's scary for some of us to contemplate learning how to face and honestly feel our emotions. We may not be entirely convinced that this can be done without dying or wanting to hurt others. Besides, our feeling-phobic friends will surely disapprove. And some of the brothers and sisters at church might question why we've become so weak or not-nice. Those realities aren't very comforting, are they?

Before you dismiss the possibility of getting more emotionally real, I have a question for you: how's your current emotion-management-method working? Perhaps not as successfully as you think. I've already described how I tried unsuccessfully to plug my sadness leak with busyness, food, and a myriad of other emotion-blockers. But I kept leaking. And my unwillingness to leave Fantasyland and face emotional reality hurt the people I love most. Fantasies always seem to do that.

I can tell you that getting emotionally honest isn't quick or easy. But I can also tell you that it is possible. We really *can* learn consistently (but not perfectly) to be angry without sinning. We really *can* deeply, genuinely grieve past and present losses, but do it differently than people who have no sure hope of comfort in Christ. And we really *can* acknowledge the reality of fear, while simultaneously choosing to trust God anyway.[6]

As we practice these, and other, new skills, we will get off the roller coaster of emotional instability. We will become more authentic, more fully alive. And we will live more consistently in the peace that Jesus promised.

Think about It

Write the words or phrases that describe your "gut-level" response to the statement: "Jesus came to take away my sins, not my feelings."

What emotions have you sometimes/often wished Jesus (or someone or something) would magically take away from you?

What do you use to block awareness of those feelings? Do you see any evidence that your attempts to make those feelings disappear create distress in your life or in the lives of those you love?

Are you ready to ask Jesus to help you honestly face and appropriately control your distressing emotions? If not, why not? If so, what are some human resources that can help you? When will you begin using them? (Remember, the more unhealthy your birth family, the more you will need compassionate support as you begin to experience the authentic emotions you have likely kept controlled out of your awareness.)

Pray about It

DEAR LORD, I know You created me to experience a lot of different feelings. But You know that some of these emotions scare me because I seem to hurt myself or others when I feel them. As usual, when I try to take control, I only make matters worse. Please teach me how to be *real* about my feelings without being *ruled* by my feelings. AMEN.

Learn More about It

Often our emotions rise and fall in response to what's happening in our most significant relationships. And our emotion-laden interpersonal connections also seem to urge us to bring out our magic wands. In the next chapter, we'll see how that works.

EIGHT

Illusions of Control in Relationships

God loves you and Sandy has a wonderful plan for your life!

I'll confess I usually approached my family and closest friends from precisely that perspective. So I think it's safe to say I understand something about how, to one degree or another, illusions of control creep into all our important relationships.

People express relational control fantasies in nearly as many ways as there are people. But these attempts to control all try to magically fulfill the human longing for interpersonal intimacy in ways that both guarantee complete relational satisfaction and eliminate all relational pain.

ILLUSIONS OF CONTROLLED INTIMACY

In his book, *False Intimacy,* Dr. Harry Schaumburg describes the roots of our personal and relational plights.

> Since the Fall, all of us have experienced loneliness . . . [and] a distortion and an agonizing disruption of intimacy. Each of us longs to break through the limitations of our existence into a blissful, unending intimacy with others. Such a dream cannot, however, be fulfilled. So we desensitize our hunger and thirst for the pre-fallen state by preoccupying ourselves with career, family, food, sex, leisure, and other distractions. But no diversions can richly satisfy our souls. *Inner emptiness, the result of original sin, lies just below the surface of the illusions we create in order to cope with life*[1] (emphasis added).

Schaumburg's book focuses on the struggles of those who use sexual intensity to create illusions of relational intimacy. We need to be clear, however, that intimacy is not synonymous with sexuality.

Ideally, each of us will have several genuinely intimate relationships in addition to a larger circle of friends, acquaintances, coworkers, etc. Ideally too, an adult expresses *sexualized* intimacy only with his or her own spouse. That's still God's plan despite prevailing cultural mores.

In genuinely intimate relationships we will risk being real about who we are with another person who will do the same. Intimacy grows over time in an atmosphere of mutual respect and shared responsibility that fosters appropriate trust. "Instant intimacy" is every bit as much an oxymoron as "jumbo shrimp." It takes time for anyone to establish a consistent (but not perfect) pattern of reliability.

In truly intimate relationships, both people know they will be emotionally and physically safe. This means that, while the other person will sometimes disappoint and/or unintentionally hurt us, we won't be subjected to ongoing disrespect or any form of physical intimidation.

As you can imagine, attempts to control others sabotage authentically intimate relationships. No one feels free to be real about personal opinions, strengths, or struggles with people who want to use him or her to plug the holes in their souls, so to speak. The healthier and more well-balanced people are, the more they will back away from efforts to subtly manipulate or blatantly control them.

Of course, for us lifelong overcontrollers, it's pretty scary to think about relating to someone without cranking-up our magic acts. So about now we may be thinking something like this:

> Sandy, you don't understand. They might not like me if I don't use my well-worn "dog and pony show" guaranteed to impress and win approval. Besides, who's to say that just being myself will be enough to make them want to get and stay closely connected to me? That's a risk I'm not sure I want to take.

To avoid this risk, the sex-obsessed adults Schaumburg describes manufactured a false intimacy using pictures, actors in porn videos, or prostitutes. In the worse case scenario, these adults used children to satisfy their longings to feel closely connected to another human being they can completely control. Instead of facing the inevitable pain inherent in real intimacy between two fallen human beings, these men and women settled for illusional pseudo-relationships with someone (or something) they could control.

I believe that the desire to avoid pain is a natural, human response designed to help us take care of our physical bodies. But just as sin created unavoidable problems and pain in our *bodies,* it also introduced unavoidable problems and pain into our *relationships.* When we insist on denying either sin-rooted reality, we actually set ourselves up for enormous, additional, and *substantially avoidable,* pain.

The more we work to create our own illusional world of pain-free, false intimacy, the farther we move from the problem-laden reality in which we actually live. So, instead of facing our real relational struggles, we retreat from all that unpleasant and sometimes painful stuff into a magical kingdom where we feel in control and safe. And these build-it-yourself relational realms use many activities other than sex to fashion fantasies of problem-free, painless intimacy. However their architects discover these illusions usually collapse. That's what brought Chuck to see me a few years ago.

Chuck was an energetic, young physician who spent nearly every waking hour with people who needed his medical skills. Yet he often became immobilized by depression and a deep sense of isolation.

Chuck said, "I guess a lot of people look up to me or appreciate what I do. But I can't think of one single soul who really knows or loves me. Not one." He told me that his intelligence and scientific interest alienated him from most of his peers when he was a child. At the same time, those traits brought praise from his parents and teachers.

As we talked together, Chuck recognized that his desire to protect himself from being hurt again pushed him to withdraw from potentially intimate relationships. He began to see how he had designed his daily schedule to preclude time for building real friendships. Chuck also looked down the road and shuddered at the prospect of living his entire life by the bump-and-run relational rule he'd been following.

Chuck expected his patients' appreciation and his colleagues accolades would keep him safe from both loneliness and relational disappointments. Can you recognize the misbelief underlying this approach to Chuck's interactions? It goes something like this: "I can control how others relate to me so I will never be lonely or hurt." Sounds familiar, doesn't it? Indeed, it's simply a variation of the basic lie behind magical-thinking's control fantasies: I can be good enough to stay safe and get loved.

Living that lie leads to relationships where we don't so much have friends as we take hostages. Talk about codependency!

CODEPENDENCY AS OVERDEPENDENCY

Like you, I've heard an awful lot of talk about codependency in the past few years. I've even written a bit about it in each of my books and have acquired quite a collection of codependency stories. For instance, you may have heard about the young woman who realized she was in a codependent relationship with her boyfriend when she had a near-death experience and *his* life flashed before her eyes.

Recently, however, critics from various quarters have consigned codependency to the trash heap of faddish jargon. Certainly we can agree that the word *codependency* has become clichéd from overuse. Meanwhile, the problem of unhealthy, overdependent relationships — whatever we call them — continues to plague the human family.

In an earlier book I defined codependency as: "a shame-based, painful pattern of dependency on others to provide a sense of personal safety, identity, and worth."[2] I still believe that describes the dynamics of the codependent/overdependent relational style. But after giving it some thought, I've concluded that that definition missed the heart of the matter. I now think that, more than anything else, *codependency/ overdependency is a pagan religion. It promotes the worship of other peoples' opinions.*

Jesus spoke directly to this issue nearly 2,000 years ago when He described the religious leaders of His day in John 12:43. He said, "they loved the approval of [others] rather than the approval of God." The *New International Version* translates that verse, "they loved the praise from [others] more than praise from God." Either way, that verse goes to the very heart of overdependent relating.

The Holy Spirit of God used John 12:43 to perform some open-heart, spiritual surgery on me a few years ago. I was forced to face my own overdependent relational pattern and life-dominating approval addiction. And it was not a pretty picture, believe me! I saw for the first time how often I enthroned others' opinions of me as god in my life.

> For if I am *overly* dependent on others for my sense of significance and security, I will inevitably be *less* dependent upon God—the true source of eternal well-being.

At the time I would have vehemently denied this, of course, while passionately proclaiming my devotion to living for Christ and His "well done." And I meant that as sincerely then as I do today. But I did not realize that, while I longed for *God's* approval, I lived the nitty-gritty dailyness of my existence looking for *people's* approval. I depended on their affirming words, satisfied smiles, and appreciative nods to keep me feeling good about myself and safe from abandonment.

Now this may seem very odd, but at that time I truly believed God expected me to live in such a way that I would please and/or impress other people so that they would like me and He would be proud that I belonged to Him. I know my mother certainly expected that. And as a child, it seemed to me that *her* expectations had such an aura of divine authenticity about them that they became *God's* expectations. Believing *that,* I also believed, of course, that mother and God wouldn't expect this unless I was able to do it. If I worked hard—or harder. Or my very, very hardest!

Like me, as a child you may have learned this overdependent way of connecting with people. If so, you're apt to notice a strong family resemblance in some of your relational control fantasies.

OVERDEPENDENCY AND ILLUSIONS OF CONTROL

To some degree, *all of our adult relationships are family reunions.*

Usually without realizing it, we search for people who resemble our earliest and *most* "significant others"—our folks or other important adults from our childhood. Each of these family-reunion type relationships offers us another chance to rewrite the original childhood drama with a happier ending. We hope we will be able to control it better this time so we finally earn some approval. (Or *more* approval.) Sometimes we persuade ourselves that *enough* approval will magically become genuine love. (Sort of like ancient alchemists' promises to transform base metals into gold.) And then we'll finally, truly feel good enough to be loveable.

Protecting ourselves with magical fantasies is like trying to keep warm in a snowstorm, wearing only "the Emperor's new clothes." The new clothes were not real. Neither are our fantasies. In some situations, they are downright dangerous.

For example, when adult sexual-abuse survivors operate from the control fantasies spun by magical thinking, they often wear loose or baggy clothing to conceal the contours of their bodies. If they still believe that the shape of their bodies caused "that basically nice person" to molest them, they think they will make interactions with potential perpetrators come out differently this time by hiding their shapeliness. These same shapelessly-clothed incest survivors, however, may screen-out awareness of sexually-unsafe situations that make them sitting ducks for rape and other forms of sexual abuse. That's the problem with self-protective fantasies. They don't protect us at all. In fact, they can put us at high risk.

You've probably figured out that the loosely-clothed incest survivors are relating from a shame-based mindset. But we've already learned that adults don't have to have been sexually abused as children to share that approach to relationships.

SHAME AND OVERDEPENDENCE

We will feel ineligible for mutually respectful and genuinely healthy relationships if we believe that we are uniquely flawed and worth less than other people. And that belief defines shame. In too many cases shame-bound individuals operate by an *any-relationship-is-better-than-no-relationship-at-all* perspective. Having abandoned hope for true intimacy, shame-bound people settle for illusions of interpersonal closeness crafted by their control fantasies.

When we relate to others based on shame and illusions of control, we're apt to feed ourselves a steady diet of mental junk food. (We acquired the taste for it as young children and probably don't know anything healthier is available.) It's packaged in statements such as these:

- "If I am good enough (meaning *flawless*), everyone I know will like/love me."
- "If there are problems in any of my relationships, it's because of something I did or failed to do."
- "I should make/keep everyone around me happy, and if I try hard enough I can."

Or perhaps our rotten relational thoughts sound more like this:

- "Others should be kind to me/make me happy/take care of me."
- "If others really cared, they would know what I want/need and give it to me."
- "If there are problems in any of my relationships, it's because of something others did or failed to do."

Obviously these statements sound very different from the previous ones. That's because overdependent relational controlling comes in two styles. As we discovered in chapter 1 when we looked at uses of personal power, we may swing from one style to the other in different situations.

Let's take a closer look at the two overcontrolling styles and the family dynamics that shaped them. (Of course our individual temperaments and traits influence us too.)

ACTIVE CONTROLLING: OVER-RESPONSIBLE RESCUERS

While researching my doctoral dissertation, I read about the roles children play in alcoholic families.[3] I learned that usually the oldest child finds a white hat labeled "Family Hero" hanging on his or her bassinet. In reality, I learned about the hero role decades earlier. Firsthand. And as a counselor, I've also learned that nearly *all* poorly functioning families, alcoholic or not, cast one of their oldest children in this appearance-preserving part.

The Family Hero, sometimes called the Responsible One, is a

high-achieving, pseudo-mature, parent-like child. Kind of a short adult, really. Here are some of their typical traits.

1. Believes he or she is "good" only when doing something for someone.
2. Learns to give orders; helps parents control younger children.
3. Needs perfection; average isn't good enough. Makes high grades.
4. Receives praise for behaving older than real age, and often feels more comfortable around adults than around children of his or her own age.
5. Becomes very organized and scheduled; takes control in crises.
6. Feels for, and focuses on helping others; unaware of own limits and needs.
7. Believes that asking for help shows weakness.

Over-responsible heroes, of course, are supposed to rescue the poorly functioning family from the shame of parental problems by achieving so much that everyone in or outside the family will think it must be healthy. The thinking seems to go like this, "Any family that can produce a kid like this must be pretty darn OK." So the Over-responsible child earns and maintains "Hero" status by working to make parents and siblings feel good, or at least better, about being part of their particular family.

When we've been taught in childhood that we could, and *should,* spend our energies changing people for the better, it's really not surprising that we continue to do exactly that as adults. The defensive roles we learned as kids to cope with the instability in our families usually become the basis for our senses of identity and the templates for all our relationships. And at this point in our lives, we may be actively controlling because we can't imagine relating any other way. For extremely overdependent, active-controllers, even contemplating a more balanced, mutually responsible relational style triggers fear of abandonment.

No matter how capable and high-achieving we may become, we actively-controlling rescuers usually feel ineligible for mutually respectful and genuinely healthy relationships. (Of course we don't say this to ourselves in so many words. We just live it.) That's part of the hurtful heritage from our shame-based families. When we've been cast as an over-responsible hero, we active-controllers compensate for a sense of shame by "saving" desperately needy victims as a way to earn the right to relate.

In effect we're saying to the needy folks in our lives, "Lucky you. I'm here now so everything is going to be all right. I'll take care of you no matter what you need. And, hey, what a great deal for you. I don't have any needs of my own. No, really. Don't worry about me. Too late? Too early? No problem. Call anytime you need me. And, above all, please, *please need me!*"

I was appalled when I stopped rescuing long enough to think deeply about what this relational attitude conveys. I had been representing myself as a being who could meet all the needs of others, yet have no needs of my own. In other words, I acted as if I were both all-sufficient and self-sustaining. Those are *God's* attributes, not mine!

Maybe this active-controlling, over-responsible-rescuer approach to relationships seems as strange to you as salmon in the Sahara. You'd rather let life and relationships take you where they will. I'm guessing that you identified with the belief statements characterizing passive-controllers.

PASSIVE CONTROLLING: UNDER-RESPONSIBLE VICTIMS

Perhaps the white hat was taken by the time you were born. If so, and if your family was significantly dysfunctional, you may have been handed a script for the role of Scapegoat/Under-reponsible One—complete with black hat. The Under-responsible One functions in the family to take the blame for problems that become too obvious to hide.

In less severely troubled families, the same birth position may have cast you in the role of "Adjuster" (also called the "Lost Child"). Again, we must not minimize the contribution of personal temperament and genetic endowment in this childhood role business. And many of us find that, over the years, we've switched back and forth between roles in our families.

The following attributes represent a combination of the less extreme traits attributed to children in the Under-responsible and Adjuster roles:

1. Receives little attention unless he/she is ill or in trouble.
2. Feels unloved and as if he/she doesn't fit into the family.
3. Stuffs feelings; builds walls.

4. Is socially immature; apt to be a loner.
5. Doesn't like routine or rules.
6. Gives up easily; is an average or below student regardless of IQ and often is not involved in school activities.
7. Has difficulty making friends so is willing to do almost anything for friendship.

I think that what I am calling the passive-controlling style of overdependent relating characterizes most of the adults who played the role of Under-responsible One or Adjuster in childhood. Many of these people also experienced some degree of physical and/or sexual abuse. Nearly all received verbal and emotional battering.

If these experiences and traits seem to fit, you've likely learned to feel safest by trying to *passively* control your relationship. To others, you may appear anything *but* controlling because you don't use the frequently obvious tactics of active-controllers. In fact, you may have a reputation for being "very accomodating" or even "so submissive." But you've learned how to establish and sustain relationships based on the under-responsible position.

After all, whichever overdependent relating style — or combination of styles — we favor, our goal is avoiding the pain that comes with genuine intimacy while also staying connected enough to others to avoid loneliness and feelings of abandonment. And passive-controllers know from experience that, if you are confused, troubled, or needy enough, you can often reach that self-protective goal thanks to all of us active-controllers who need your neediness to reach that same goal ourselves.

RELATIONAL PROBLEMS
CAUSED BY OVERCONTROLLING

As we're learning, we do not have the magical power to really control other people. Living that fairy tale creates major problems guaranteed to short-circuit healthy, authentic interpersonal connections. Let's look at three of the most common problems.

Problem #1:
Controlling and Boundaries

Our shame-based and self-protective overdependency and fear of abandonment usually get in the way of setting appropriate personal boundaries. Some of us may be like the young woman from an unhealthy family who asked me how she could get a married coworker to leave her alone without "getting him angry," as she put it. She was crushed when I said that she could either set an appropriate relational boundary with her coworker or try to control his response to her. But not both.

We need to face the real possibility that our boundary setting efforts won't be greeted warmly by those we've allowed to disrespect us in the past. Unless we're willing to retire the "anything-goes-because-I'm-so-caring" routines we've used to control other people's feelings toward us, we can not effectively set personal boundaries with them.

For example, adults raised in alcoholic families are often attracted to alcoholics they want to help. Many of these adults endure degrading and even dangerous situations "in the name of love" as they attempt to save the alcoholic by controlling his or her drinking. The help-aholics determined to improve the alcoholics often say something like, "I wouldn't want him/her to think I don't care." These same sincere adults nearly always describe feeling "out of control" in their relationships with the alcoholics they seek to rescue. In reality, they have voluntarily relinquished their control, along with their personal boundaries, all because of the erroneous belief that they could, or should, control another adult.

Problem #2:
Controlling and Relational Honesty

Wanting someone to change isn't necessarily a problem. But trying to *make* them change usually is. Often our shame-based insecurities propel us into frantic efforts to make our friends (and especially our spouses) see things our way. It's as if we believe that we can be truly close only if we and our family or closest friends become clones. From this perspective, different tastes and separate opinions seem dangerous. If we tend toward passive controlling, we may protect ourselves by abdicating our true tastes and opinions. Active-controllers usually try to alter the tastes and opinions of others. With the first option, we disrespect ourselves and undercut the genuine intimacy we crave. And we eventually feel resentment about "not being able to be myself." The second approach disrespects others and typically leads to mutual frustration.

Problem #3:
Controlling and Unbalanced Relationships

Our illusional style of control creates unhealthy, unbiblical, and un-balanced relational roles that need to be filled. So over-responsible, active-controlling rescuers must find folks who will play victims. And under-responsible, passive-controlling victims always need rescuers. Playing either role disrespects everyone involved, destroys genuine intimacy, and disregards biblical guidelines.

The New Testament uses the words *one another* several times to describe ideal relationships between believers. As those words imply, people in one-anothering relationships take mutual responsibility to follow Scriptural principles. When they do, their thoughts, actions, and *interactions* will be consistently balanced and healthy. (They will become more and more consistent as they mature cognitively, emo-tionally, and spiritually, but will never be perfect.)

So if one person is consistently thoughtless, even self-absorbed, and the other is expected to be kind and forgiving, their relationship clearly lacks one-anothering. I've noticed a curious thing in such relationships among some religious folk. If the kind/forgiving ones wise-up and try to change the relationships, the thoughtless/self-absorbed ones frequently use verses like Ephesians 4:32. That verse instructs Christians to be kind, tender-hearted, and forgiving to *one another.* However, the unrepentently thoughtless/self-absorbed one will point to that verse and say, "See. It says right here you're sup-posed to forgive and be kind to me."

This relational principle also means that if we have a relation-ship in which I consistently insist on playing the all-knowing, ever-competent "stronger" one, and you consistently play the all-befud-dled, never-competent "weaker" one, neither of us is one-anothering. We're both denying the truth about our humanity which says we *each* have strengths and weaknesses. By the way, this particular imbalanced, unbiblical relational pattern characterizes many of us people helpers. We often find it extremely difficult to let others help and minister to us even in times of genuine need. Vivian certainly did.

"I never let friends help me, even when I could really use it. But I'm always there for them no matter what." That's how Vivian, a well-respected, twenty-eight-year-old pediatric nurse described her rela-tionships. As we talked about the scriptural principle of one-anothering, her brow furrowed and she looked confused. "I don't know if I even *want* to relate that way, to tell you the truth. I feel really weak and embarrassed just thinking about asking friends for help or anything. I guess that sounds weird since I'm always trying to convince them to accept help from me. I mean, aren't Christians supposed to be helpful?"

I asked Vivian to read and meditate upon the relational principle found in Galatians 6:2 and 6:5. Those verses tell believers both to "carry each other's burdens" and that "each one should carry his [or her] own load." Vivian was amazed that, instead of contradicting each other, those two verses provided balance in human interactions. They tell Christians to handle the normal "loads" of life without being dependent on others, but they also exhort believers to be willing to give and receive help in overburdening circumstances. That principle reflects the real lives of real people who are capable of managing routine responsibilities themselves but occasionally face crises when they need temporary help. This depicts healthy interdependence.

SURRENDERING RELATIONAL CONTROL AND CARES

Healthy interdependence. Now there's an interesting concept! For us overdependent overcontrollers, it remains only a concept until we relinquish the illusion that we can change and control others.

For decades, Al-Anon has used the phrase "Loving Detachment" to describe the relational goal for people dedicated to rescuing alcoholics. This relational approach permits us to regain respect for the person we have been trying to change. When we detach, we no longer attempt to control the person or his/her problems.

Christians find scriptural counsel to go one step further. In 1 Peter 5:7, we're told to cast all our cares on our caring God. Many of us have a history of taking one or more individuals, and *their* cares, and making them *our* cares. If so, we need to purposefully, lovingly detach those cares from our shoulders and cast them on God. He not only cares far more than we, but He is also wise enough to know what to do with them.

That doesn't sound very loving if we've been taught that *rescue* is a synonym for *love*. But it's not. I believe the most truly loving approach we can take toward those we value includes stepping down off the thrones of their universe. We need to let God be God in the lives of the people for whom we seek the best. But we will never do that until we take others off *our* thrones. Only then will we experience the truth that God can fill our deepest longings for intimate attachment. Only then will we trust God to do that for those we love.

Think about It

Do you believe "closeness" equals "sameness" in important relationships?

Read Romans 14, especially verses 1, 13, and 19. What do those verses say about letting others have their own opinions?

To whom do you look for guidance, help, and comfort? An individual, or God? (Your answer will tell you who *really* gets to be God in your life.)

Are you ready to purposefully release your "control captives" into God's care? If so, read 1 Peter 5:7, substituting for the words "all your care" (KJV) or "anxiety" (NIV) the name(s) of the person(s) you are "casting" upon God's care.

Here's an example of how one creative counselee wrote this exercise in her personal journal: "I'm hereby casting _____ and all my anxiety about _____ on You, Lord, because I believe You care about _____ as much as You care about me."

What name(s) could you use in that statement? Will you sincerely write something like that statement including that/those name(s)? If not, why not?

Pray about It

DEAR LORD, Please help me trust You enough to put You on the throne of my life, not just for eternal salvation, but also for daily direction. And please show me how to stop trying to take Your place in people's lives. Thank You for being such a patient teacher and loving guide. AMEN

Learn More about It

Many of us have found to our sorrow that illusions of relational control spill over into our roles as spouses and parents. We'll look at how that can work out next.

N I N E

Illusions of Control within Families

When it comes to our families, many of us face one of two situations that would drive any self-respecting illusionist wild.

In some of the relationships with our spouses and/or children we attempt to pull rabbits out of hats, so to speak. We keep performing cognitive gymnastics, jumping through behavioral hoops, and twisting ourselves into emotional pretzels to create the illusion of family harmony, marital commitment, etc. But we don't have the power to produce something from nothing.

In other family relationships, instead of trying to pull a rabbit from an empty hat, we see a rabbit that's not supposed to be there. We frantically crank up the smoke machine so no one in the audience will notice the embarrassing bunny. These unwelcomed "rabbits" could be the truth about family secrets or the choices made by spouses or children or a dozen other things. And to make this rabbit-hunting and rabbit-hiding business even crazier, we usually do both at the same time!

In this chapter we'll see several ways in which illusions of control impact marriage and raising children. Since whole books address each of these relationships, we obviously will just skim the surface. Let's begin by examining an illusion about what constitutes a family.

ILLUSIONS OF CONTROL AND FAMILY PRESERVATION

Despite the rise of unwed, drug-addicted teen mothers and fathers who neglect and often horribly abuse their children, some social service agencies operate from a fantasyland ideal that equates giving birth with parenting. This concept is called "family preservation." However, wanting something to be so does not make it so. And trying to create the illusion of family structure where none exists can spell disaster.

We have all read about children being taken from inadequate parents. In many cases, the youngsters are returned to the same parents by well-meaning agencies who invest substantial time and money to help preserve the family. Despite these investments, too often the parents subsequently maim, molest, and/or murder their children. Opponents of the family preservation concept contend that this practice

> rewards criminal and irresponsible behavior and conduct, but more importantly it's trying to bribe people into being what they can't be. We see children die, children get horribly abused.[1]

Critics also theorize that agency officials' concerns over tight budgets and heavy caseloads often outweigh the needs of the children. I don't know about that. But I think the comment quoted above suggests another reason the children were returned to their abusive parents. We want to believe that biological parents, especially mothers, will always care for their children if given half a chance. Can you hear the magical thinking? This variation says, "We can control these abusive parents' treatment of their children if we supply enough money and encouragement." Sadly, this worthwhile objective overlooks the reality that we cannot make people be what they will not choose to be.

Obviously, with the number of tragedies reported in foster care situations, judges and child protection workers must choose between two blatantly imperfect and potentially dangerous alternatives when it comes to placing neglected and abused children.

I know it's a stretch, but I see similarities between the magical thinking and illusions of control in the "family preservation" concept and those in some far more respectable-looking homes. Even religious homes.

ILLUSIONS OF
MARRIAGE MAKEOVERS

Hundreds of volumes have been written about marriage and divorce. So I have no illusion that I can do more than touch on a few issues specifically related to control fantasies.

Ideally, before we marry, we should take time to get to know a prospective spouse, seek God's guidance, get wise premarital counseling, and pursue a host of other activities which will positively influence marital success. In addition, those of us who harbor persistent control fantasies about our power to change people need to ask ourselves four questions before marriage.

1. Am I willing to spend my life with this person if he or she never changes from the way he or she is at this very moment?
2. Would I want to become more like this person just as she or he is right now?
3. Would I want this person, just as he or she is now, to be the father/mother of my children?
4. Would I want my children to be just like this person as she or he is right now?[2]

Of course, most of us didn't know enough about ourselves or our relational patterns to ask such questions. As a result, many of us carried more than Grandma's silver or Uncle Joe's toolbox into our marriages. We brought with us a mentality of magical makeovers. In extreme cases, some of us may even try to make over genuinely dangerous and severely disturbed persons into sorely misunderstood and slightly difficult ones. Whatever the details and degree of dysfunction in one or both spouses, these illusions of control express the belief that, "I'll take you as you are right now because I believe I can magically make you over into what I need you to be to plug the hole in my soul."

Because so *few* people take the time to consider questions like the four above, so *many* marriages sooner or later end in divorce. What a tragedy!

DIVORCE AND ILLUSIONS OF CONTROL

Do you remember what Peter Pan told the lost children to do when Tinker Bell was dying? He said, "If you believe in fairies, clap your hands." And as the children chanted, "I do believe in fairies, I do believe in fairies," they clapped furiously. Of course the magic worked. Tinker Bell was saved from the brink of death. What always works in Never-Never Land, however, rarely succeeds in real life.

I've observed more than a few sincere Christian spouses attempt to, in effect, chant and clap their marriages back to life while their partners pursued divorce. The divorce-resisting spouses learned that, even when they did everything they could to save their marriages, they did not have the power to accomplish that feat singlehandedly. Insisting that *one* Christian spouse can pray away or work hard enough to prevent the death of a marriage denies the power of the other spouse's choices. This Peter Pan approach to marriage preservation reminds me of a story I read recently.

Because *real* people in *real* communities die, governments zone land for cemeteries; however, in one of America's poshest ski-resorts, the reality of death has been zoned away. Listen to the explanation by the editor of the town's newspaper. "A cemetery in Vail is against what Vail is all about. People come here to have a good time and ski and enjoy the atmosphere. I think a cemetery for Vail is counterproductive."[3] Talk about illusions of control: if we have no place to bury people, no one will die here!

ILLUSIONS VERSUS REALITY IN CHRISTIANS' MARRIAGES AND DIVORCES

In this real and sinful world, real and sinful spouses have marital problems. Sometimes these problems are so severe that one or both spouses seek to end the marriage. To be sure, God desires marriages to last "as long as you both shall live." Nevertheless, God allows people to make choices even when they violate His will and produce destructive consequences.

Along with a lot of other things like lying tongues and oppressing the weak, God hates divorce. And any way you look at it, divorce is a failure. It's not the unpardonable sin, but it wreaks devastating pain upon everyone involved, especially the least responsible—children. And since marriage is a metaphor for the relationship of Christ to His church, divorce destroys the earthly shadow of that divine reality. No wonder God hates divorce.

Now the truth is that people die—even in Vail, Colorado. And marriages involving Christians die—even in your church and mine. If churches want to preserve the illusion that divorce happens only among unbelievers, then they won't plan any programs to support, encourage, or comfort the spouses and children wounded by the shrapnel of exploding marriages. That's about as realistic as outlawing cemeteries.

Of course, churches willing to face the often unpleasant reality of ministering to real sinners, redeemed or not, would also provide a variety of marriage-*building* resources. For example, churches could begin at junior high school level teaching biblical principles for relating in general as well as relating in male-female relationships. Bible studies and fellowship groups for single adults could focus on those same subjects in addition to marriage-preparation issues. And married adults of all ages need frequent instruction and encouragement to keep Christ on the throne in their hearts and homes. They can get that through sermon series, special seminars, Bible studies, small groups, and a myriad of other methods.

All of these marriage-preserving programs represent a more realistic response to the real needs of real people than the standard, two- or three-session premarital counseling churches typically offer. Sadly, churches intent on fostering the illusion that Christians just need to read their Bibles and pray more to solve all their personal and marital problems aren't likely to consider implementing any of those suggestions.

As I write this, my husband and I will soon celebrate our thirty-seventh wedding anniversary. Believe me, we've worked through lots of annoying differences as well as a few very serious difficulties. Needless to say, we wouldn't have made it this far without our stubborn commitment to marriage and an abundance of God's grace. (Not necessarily in that order.) As an evangelical Christian, and a recovering approval-addict who is committed to marriage, I have been very reluctant to write the previous few pages lest they be mistaken for an apologetic supporting divorce. Nothing could be further from the truth. However, I *do* support facing reality rather than living in illusion.

THE HIGH COST OF MARITAL ILLUSIONS

We've already seen the tragedies that result from pretending, in the name of family preservation, that a zero-parent home is safe and stable. I've begun to suspect that something disquietingly similar goes on in some churchgoing, so-called Christian families. Although it may be difficult to imagine, I've learned (decades after the fact) of situations where one spouse allows the other to sexually and/or physically batter one or more of their children. Why? Because the consenting spouse was determined "to save the marriage at any cost." That appearance-preserving goal outweighed concerns for the children who were forced to pay the price.

Am I saying those consenting spouses should have immediately pursued divorce? First of all, they should have pursued safety for their children, even if that meant separating from the offending spouse and pressing charges. And it usually does. I see divorce as the absolutely last resort after exhausting all resources to influence a battering spouse to repent, accept the consequences of his/her sinful choices, get help to change, and submit to accountability relationships to monitor that change. I believe this also applies to marriages where *spouses* are battered instead of children.

It isn't that divorce is a solution for illusional marriages any more than foster care solves the problems of illusional parenting. In both cases, each alternative contains painful realities and potential tragedies. In truth, those are the only kind of alternatives available when spouses and parents continue to sin against God, their mates, and their children. So let's not succumb to the illusion that being forced to choose the lesser of two wrongs ever creates a situation as right as what could have been if the spouses and parents had chosen repentance and restoration.

We magical-thinking types don't perform our hunt-the-rabbit, hide-the-rabbit routines only on the marital stage. We take the show on the road, as it were. Throughout this book we've focused on how we use our magical people-controlling acts to earn assurance of our parents' approval and love. But it doesn't stop there. When *we* have children, many of us move our control fantasies into the nursery right along with the stuffed animals.

ILLUSIONS OF CONTROL
IN OUR PARENTING

Anything that begins with the word labor *can't be easy!*

Parenting challenges the best in us and too often brings out the worst. Christian parents will be driven to their knees on behalf of their children time and time again. At least that's been my experience. To be honest, many of those prayers were more about my struggles to be a good parent than my children's struggles to be good kids. (My husband and I have told Dave and Becky, and anyone else who'd listen, that we think our children have been incredible blessings in our lives.)

Most of my parenting struggles directly related to my illusions of control, coupled with a giant, industrial-strength addiction to performance-based approval. Whatever particular spin our personalities and personal histories put on our control fantasies, we need to take seriously their potential to wound our children — literally and figuratively.

Many authorities believe that the need to feel in control lies at the heart of child beating, just as it does in the case of spouse battering. Thankfully, most of us would never consider physically pummeling our children. Nevertheless, we can still hurt them with our persistent determination to control nearly everything about them, even things as basic as an infant's appetite.

Recently, I read about parenting education materials that teach, among other things, the necessity of "parent-controlled" feeding schedules for newborns. Through books, tapes, and church-based seminars, parents learn to view demand feeding as part of "a philosophy that denies man is made in the image of God and now exists in the condition of depravity."[4]

I must say I was surprised by that concept. I firmly believe in the doctrine of pervasive human depravity, yet I never considered my newborn's cries of hunger to be evidence of that sad state. And I've always thought that so-called "demand feeding" was based on the idea that infants know more about when they are hungry than their caregivers.

I suspect that the authors of this material sincerely seek to counterbalance the permissive child-rearing philosophy so prevalent in our culture. In the same way, many of us who grew up in chaotic, unstable families are determined to bring control and order into our homes now. They and we can easily swing from one extreme to the other.

The more out-of-control we feel in some area of our lives, the more apt we are to use our children as proof that at least we can control *something*. And let's face it, kids are so much more controllable than adults. So they offer a major temptation for insecure, over-controllers. In the next few pages we'll examine two parenting areas where we're most likely to succumb to that temptation.

Illusions of Control and Discipline

"Discipline your son, and he will give you peace; he will bring delight to your soul," advises Proverbs 29:17 (NIV). And Dr. T. Berry Brazelton, Professor Emeritus of Pediatrics at Harvard Medical School agrees. (Not that Scripture needs human agreement to validate its truth.) "Don't be afraid to discipline your child. . . . By setting rules and expectations, you teach him to respect society's limits,"[5] says the renowned childcare specialist.

I doubt any of us would argue with either the biblical insight or Brazelton's statement. But we might have some lively disagreements about just exactly what constitutes discipline, especially since those of us with overcontrolling tendencies often express them in two disciplining extremes with our children.

Overcontrolling Children's Behavior

Some overcontrolling parents seem to focus on their children's *behavior* in an effort to eliminate any element the parent deems unacceptable. This approach easily overlooks the motives and goals *behind* a child's behavior. In many cases, the motives and goals behind *our* overcontrolling efforts spring from our shame-driven desires to create the image of being a perfect parent by creating a perfectly controlled child.

We're likely to use with our children what our parents used with us to enforce behavioral rules. And if our parents *failed* to consistently enforce appropriate rules, that can produce an overcontrolling rebound response, so to speak, when we become parents. Sharon learned that.

Sharon and Jess came for counseling because they often argued about how to raise their children. They loved Jesus, each other, and their two preadolescent daughters. But they couldn't agree about what was good for them. Jess came from a secure and loving home where he learned how to have fun as well as how to work hard. Sharon, however, was raised with an emotionally immature mother and a series of stepfathers who provided little or no family stability.

Jess explained his view of their problem: "I know Sharon's really a super mom in many ways. I just worry that she's way too rigid with the girls. I want to stand behind Sharon's decisions, but honestly I think she's way out of line sometimes. So I don't, and that causes more arguments."

Sharon explained: "Jess can't understand how hard I try to have some routine and order. In my family, I never knew what to expect from one minute to the next. Everybody knows routine is important for kids. Jess would let the girls goof-off all the time."

Over time, Sharon saw that her desire to enforce inflexible schedules for her daughters' homework, music lessons, soccer practices, and chores left very little time for them to have relaxed fun. And Jess learned that his efforts to smuggle playtime into his girls' strictly scheduled lives only influenced Sharon to exert even more rigid control. Things improved slowly as Jess and Sharon practiced switching their customary strict-one, lax-one roles. They also worked together to reorchestrate the rhythm of the family's routine.

Like many adults raised in poorly-functioning families, Sharon had learned to invest her energy in externals such as appearance, behavior, and achievement—her own and her children's. Sharon has lots of company.

Emphasizing Externals

I think that many parents focus on controlling their children for the purpose of promoting achievement rather than instilling character. And it seems that marketing professionals have noticed this achievement orientation too. Consider this evidence. Each year the manufacturer of my daily schedule organizer sends me a notice to order the next year's product. Among the many new items featured in my latest reminder letter was a *"Student Organizer."* It was "designed especially for use from fifth grade through college." And the student organizer promised "100 percent satisfaction guaranteed." The advertisement, obviously addressed to parents, didn't say whether that guarantee applied to the student or to the organizer! (Maybe both?)

By the way, the smiling preteen girl on the ad held a test paper marked with a huge, red $A+$. I couldn't help but think how that picture panders to parents' illusions of control. The implicit message is: "Parents who purchase this product will produce kids who produce top grades."

Now, I'm all for teaching children to use time wisely. In fact, since Dave and Becky were seriously involved in competitive sports, they both had to learn to budget their time or they'd never have made it through college. And they managed to do it without an expensive schedule organizer.

Maybe I'm overreacting, but I think that having fifth-graders schedule their days in fifteen-minute increments crosses the line of good judgment and plunges into the realm of performance-focused overcontrolling. I'm guessing that a lot of achievement-oriented controllers purchased that new student organizer. (No, I did *not* include information about where to order one in the chapter notes.)

At this point, you may not be sure *where* you focus when it comes to your children. Perhaps you can get a clearer picture as you answer the following questions.

- Do I affirm and reward my child for "brave attempts" as well as for obvious successes?
- Do I emphasize building my child's character or polishing my child's performance?

Remember, in Scripture we find Jesus strongly rebuking the religious leaders of His day who emphasized outer ritual performance to the neglect of inner godly character. It's dismayingly easy for us overcontrolling parents to take the same approach with our children. And we don't even need "student organizers" to do it.

It is not easy to change deep-seated beliefs about what's most important in life, but we can do it with God's help. When we do, we will compliment our children's character traits and brave attempts. And our children will hear us commenting on their inner qualities to others as much or more than we recite their latest achievements in school, sports, business, and the like.

While many overcontrolling parents focus on strictly prescribed behavior and lofty achievements, others concentrate their effort on controlling their children's feelings—specifically feelings about *them* as parents.

Overcontrolling Children's Feelings and Approval

Standing in a store beside a preschooler who is screaming, "I hate you! I hate you for not letting me get/do [whatever]!" ranks right near the bottom of any parent's list of favorite things. And if we've looked to our offspring to provide the total, unwavering love we've failed to find in other relationships, our discipline intentions may collapse under the weight of such a momentary rage. If so, our child will hold us hostage with his or her angry pouts, copious tears, and/or dramatic declarations of abject, eternal hatred.

All this means we must commit to focusing our energies more on building our children's character than on keeping their moment-by-moment approval. That's more difficult for some of us than for others, depending on our personal histories. We may need help from a counselor and/or well-balanced and biblical parenting books, classes, and other resources. And older parents with a proven track record usually share their ideas gladly if we ask.

Clearly, we overcontrollers wrestle with finding balance in child discipline. But that's nothing compared to the knock-down-drag-out battle we may fight against the need to relinquish *all* control of our children.

ILLUSIONS OF CONTROL AND RELEASING OUR CHILDREN

Many of us have spent our lives trying to extract emotional nourishment from parents too empty to supply it. Still emotionally famished, it is temptingly easy to turn to our children for that love and closeness our parents never, or perhaps very meagerly, provided. When that scenario describes our parenting perspective, we likely experience great distress, even mild (or *not* so mild) panic, when our children begin to develop separate identities.

Overcontrolling parents face major crises when their desires to dominate their children collide head-on with their children's God-designed push for increasing individuation. (As the word implies, *individuation* is that process of gradually becoming a distinct and separate individual.) These major developmental collisions typically occur when children are toddlers, adolescents, and when they leave home. And if toddlers tap into our compulsions to control, teens can trigger veritable convulsions of overcontrolling.

It doesn't have to be that way, of course. In well-functioning families, as youngsters continue to mature, parents reciprocate by continuing to relinquish additional control and responsibility to them. Here's how this process looks graphically. (Of course, this transfer of responsibility and control process is not as uncomplicated as the un-wavering diagonal line in the chart suggests. A diagonal roller coast-er—especially during adolescence—would be closer to the truth.)

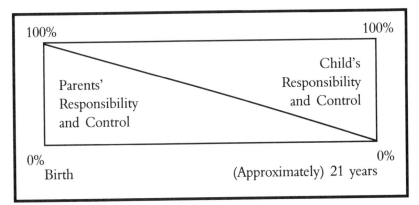

Figure 9-1

Emotionally and spiritually mature parents realize that they are fashioning wings for their children as they grow, so that one day they can fly from the family nest. But insecure, overcontrolling parents specialize in strings, not wings. They emotionally hamstring their kids to create an overdependence that allows the parents to continue overcontrolling. As we've noted before, we live what we believe. The chart on page 136 shows contrasting beliefs that we live out in our parenting as we meet our children's developmental steps with either overcontrolling strings or appropriate wings. I've also included an example of how these beliefs might be expressed.

You may have noticed that I've used the word *releasing* to de-scribe this process of gradually letting go of our children. I take that term from a word-picture found in Psalm 127:4-5 where children are compared to arrows.[6]

That strange-sounding imagery suggests several essential parenting tasks. First, archers in biblical times knew they needed to polish their arrows to minimize irregularities that might prevent the arrows from accomplishing their intended purposes. In a sense, we "polish" our children when we discipline and when we teach respon-sibility and respect for legitimate authority, for themselves, and for others. Arrows also need to be balanced so they fly straight and true. And healthy parents know we must balance discipline with encour-

---

Contrasting Approaches to Releasing Our Children

Giving "Wings"	Giving "Strings"
Underlying Belief: Parents are supposed to give their children unconditional love and wise guidance to help them become increasingly responsible for themselves, for their choices, and for their consequences. (Ideally, under the Lordship of Jesus Christ.)	*Underlying Belief:* Children are supposed to give their parents unconditional love, stay dependent upon them, and feel totally responsible for their parents' happiness so the parents stay in control and avoid feeling lonely or abandoned.
Example: When my teen consistently demonstrates trustworthiness, I grant his/her request to spend Spring Break at the beach with a close friend and his/her family.	*Example:* When my teen asks to spend Spring Break with a close friend and his/her family, I tell my child he/she is too young for that and I imply he/she is selfish for wanting to "go off so long" without me.

Figure 9-2[7]

---

agement, affirmation, and clear expressions of our love. In addition, arrows must be pointed in the right direction. When arrows fly haphazardly, tragedies can follow. Similarly, we know that we need to guide our children into right paths by teaching and modeling biblical values and by consistently and prayerfully exposing them to the message of God's redeeming love. Finally, when arrows and children have been polished, balanced, and pointed in the right direction, *we must release them.*

Even without histories of magical thinking and control fantasies, releasing our children can be frightening when we consider the condition of the world. If we're wise, this legitimate concern will drive us to our knees. And while we're praying for our children's protection and guidance, we can thank God for His assurance that He (who is in us by His Spirit) is greater than the evil one who is in the world. (See 1 John 4:4.)

It's true, there are no guarantees in marriage or in parenting because our spouses and our children are separate individuals who make choices of their own. That reality ought to call us to even more "knee bends," which are, after all, the very best exercise for true marital and parenting fitness. For when you stop to think about it, God asks us to do with our spouses and children the very thing He asks us to do with our entire lives: release them to Him and rely on His faithfulness.

Think about It

Reread the four questions on page 126. If you are single and have begun to recognize your illusions of control, write these questions on a 3x5 card and place it beside the photo of your boyfriend or girlfriend. Each time you look at the photo, ask and answer the questions again.

If you are married already, and you have begun to recognize your illusions of control, are you willing to face needed changes in the relationship? Will you talk to your spouse about these changes? If so, when? If not, why not? (Note: if you are afraid to talk to your spouse about the quality of your relationship, your marriage needs help. Now!)

Here are three questions parents need to ask themselves.

1. Is my primary goal with my children to do everything I can to make them successful so people will know I'm a good parent?
2. Am I trying to make myself indispensable in my children's lives to make up for the emptiness I've experienced in my own *adult* relationships?
3. Do my children see from my attitudes and actions that I try to control every aspect of my life despite what I profess about trusting God?[8]

Pray about It

DEAR LORD, I know that You created families. And I know You love me and my family even more than I do. Please move in the hearts of those I love so that they will be drawn more closely to You. And please continue that work in my heart too. I long for us to come closer together as we all move closer to You. AMEN

Learn More about It

Most people reading this kind of book sincerely long to develop a vibrant life of faith. Yet when it comes to our relationships with God, most of us probably can find evidence of control fantasies. If we look. We'll do just that in the next chapter.

Illusions of Control
and Fairy-tale Faith

"You are in control! So, if man has control, who no longer has it? God. . . . God cannot do anything in this earth unless we let Him."[1]

Wow! What a great deal this is. Even if I can't control my parents and other important people in my life—no problem. Because I can make God, the ultimate authority figure, give me everything I desire and long to receive. No wonder so-called "name-it-and-claim-it" preachers, like the one quoted above, have enormous followings.

Those of us who feel most powerless to control our parents' expression of love and approval may be prone to crave "signs and wonders" to reassure ourselves and show the world that God, the heavenly parent, loves us and approves of our faith. And the more out-of-control we felt in childhood and still feel as adults, the more we'll be sitting ducks for religious pitches like these.

I think such outrageously unbiblical statements contribute to a deeply disturbing trend in some circles of Christianity: confusion between creature and Creator. And I believe this is the central problem with fairy-tale faith.

FAIRY-TALE FAITH:
CONFUSING CREATURE AND CREATOR

In his excellent book, *Yearning,* pastor Craig Barnes speaks to the heretical confusion of Creator and creature.

> The forbidden tree planted in the middle of everyone's garden is a reminder that God has not revealed all of His work or plans to us.

And that can drive us wild with insecurity. . . . Unable to live with a God we cannot fully understand, and thus *can never control,* we rush to find alternative gods who promise to be more manageable (emphasis added).[2]

Barnes writes that we Christians turn to a variety of different approaches that grandiosely promise to control God for us. Many of us conservative evangelicals have believed that our rigid orthodoxy and right living, including daily devotions (using inerrant study Bibles, of course) would do the trick. Other believers have taken the charismatic route where they know they have a grip on God because they see His signs and wonders in their churches.

In this chapter we will briefly discuss both these expressions of Christian faith, focusing on their magical-thinking aspects. We'll start with the so-called health-and-wealth movement because it seems to offer more blatant examples of religiously-garbed control fantasies.

ILLUSIONS OF CONTROL IN "HEALTH-AND-WEALTH" CHRISTIANITY

In an August, 1993 *Christianity Today* article, a scholar who has followed the faith movement for a decade captures the malfunctioning heart of the problem with what is sometimes called word-of-faith, name-it-and-claim-it, or health-and-wealth Christianity.

The health and wealth gospels are, in their extreme, a symptom of a deeper problem, that being an ongoing tendency to elevate redeemed humanity at the expense of God's transcendence and sovereignty. This inclination can take its form by *placing humanity and human powers at the center of the universe,* and placing God at man's disposal (emphasis added).[3]

Anything sound familiar? You bet, it's grandiosely infantile magical thinking. And when magical thinking invades our faith, it produces a kind of dumbing-down of God and divining-up of mankind.

In extremes of magical-thinking theology, we see people "standing in faith to take dominion over the banking system" to prevent an overdrawn check from clearing. In such a situation, Christians may be seeing life more through the eyes of desperation than the eyes of faith!

"Word-of-Faith" Fantasies

"It's faith, faith, faith and no Jesus anywhere. We have to have faith in Jesus, the author and finisher of our faith. So, where do I stand on faith? Stop seeking faith and start seeking the Lord!"[4]

That's what renowned faith teacher Benny Hinn stated in mid-1993 concerning the word-of-faith movement, after being confronted about the unscriptural aspects of his preaching.

The term "word-of-faith," sometimes used to describe the health-and-wealth movement, refers to one of the movement's doctrinal cornerstones. This teaching says that faith is a force — a powerful, creative entity in itself. And words are containers that release this creative force; therefore, everything that happens to us is a result of our words. In fact, this doctrine teaches that God used His words to release the creative power of His faith to bring the world into existence. That means that it was the power of faith, *per se,* rather than God Himself that created the heavens and the earth.

What's more, this belief system states that every person can create by his or her word-of-faith when he or she has that God-kind of faith because even *God* must respond when we use it. That's the conclusion reached by health-and-wealth teachers who mistranslate Mark 11:22 so that "have faith *in* God" becomes have the faith *of* God.[5]

To make this God-like creative force even more accessible to all of us, one of the pioneers in the contemporary word-of-faith movement provides a "formula of faith." It has four simple steps: (1) say it; (2) do it; (3) receive it; and (4) tell it so others may believe.[6]

What a seductive setup for spiritually naive, insecure over-controllers! All we have to do is master God-like faith, and then we can speak whatever we want into existence *like God.* There's only one problem with this promise: it's a lie born from the union of magical control fantasies and erroneous interpretations of Scripture.

Only God speaks the creative words "let there be. . . ." in Genesis. And the Bible never uses the Hebrew word for that phrase in reference to *human* creativity. It is unique to the limitless Creator, and beyond the established limits of His creatures.[7]

The Scripture makes a very important and careful distinction between Creator and creature. That truth confronts us with the need to acknowledge our creatureliness. Of course, that means we must also embrace the truth of our limits, our neediness, and our inability to control people and events. We don't stop being creatures when we start being Christians.

That's not what a lot of us overcontrollers want to hear, is it? Especially if our relationships and lives feel distressingly out-of-control because of family conflicts, unpaid bills, dead-end jobs, and/or poor health. We want to hear promises of guaranteed success.

The Gospel of Guaranteed Success

How to Write Your Own Ticket with God.[8] That's the tantalizing title of a book authored by one of the leading spokesmen of the contemporary health-and-wealth movement. What an appealing prospect that title presents, especially to those of us with life-dominating illusions of control. We can just tell God what we want, and He'll supply it. This search for success encompasses both financial and physical problems.

Guaranteed Wealth

"How to be a Millionaire and Use the Word of God to Help You Climb." That advertisement headline probably grabbed the attention of Atlanta-area readers when it appeared on March, 1993. For a fee of $29.00 ($35.00 at the door), folks could attend a *two-and-a-half hour* seminar that promised they'd "learn how to use God's Word to" (among many other things): heal the sick; resolve disputed bills; avoid a divorce; and "move into the millionaire status." Under bold type asking **"who should attend,"** seven categories of people were listed. And in case the seminar sponsors omitted anybody, they added, "If you have any type of problem bothering you, please come!"[9] Perhaps that last sentence would have been more accurate if it had said: Anyone who wants to learn yet another way to *control God,* please come!"

Guaranteed Health

Often our longing to control God focuses more on gaining *health* than wealth. If so, we'll find plenty of preachers eager to tell us how to use our faith-filled words to guarantee our complete physical well-being. In addition many "faith healers" will be glad to use *their* faith-filled words to heal us.

You'll recall that word-of-faith leaders teach that faith is a principle or a force to which even God *must* respond. And we release this God-like and God-controlling force through our words. So when it comes to being healed, this doctrine forms a spiritual syllogism:

Premise One:	Those who confess that they are healed will be healed.
Premise Two:	Those who do not confess their healing will stay sick.
Conclusion:	Therefore all those who are not healed have made negative confessions.[10]

Now as any Logic 101 student knows, if we start with a faulty premise, we come to a faulty conclusion. And I believe that whenever we begin from the belief that we and our words have the power to eliminate all disease, we are not only functioning with a faulty premise, we are entering spiritual Fantasyland. And that's where we hear the familiar language of illusional thinking loud and clear. The health-and-wealth version says, "I can have faith enough to stay safe (healthy and wealthy) and get God's approval."

Without a doubt, God sovereignly chooses to heal physical disease apart from natural means from time to time. However, many more times He appears to allow illness to run its course — even in the bodies of believers who deeply love and trust Him. I've met some dear Christian brothers and sisters who have been, in essence, spiritually abused by sincere word-of-faith folks.

One of them was Margaret, a fortysomething homemaker who spoke to me during a conference lunch break. She said, "I really believed God would heal my diabetes. I really, really did. I threw away my insulin even though my husband had a fit. You see, I went to a healing service one of my Christian friends told me about, and they said that if I wanted God to heal me and believed that He would, I'd be healed."

Margaret's mouth twitched and her eyes became moist as she continued. "They warned me not to make a 'negative confession' by telling anybody that I still had diabetes if the symptoms tried to come back. I was supposed to stand in faith and claim my healing from God." She lowered her voice and her head to avoid my eyes and added, "But I went into a coma and my husband rushed me to the hospital. My doctor said I could have died. No one will ever know how guilty and ashamed I feel for not being able to stand in faith and keep my healing." In reality, many other spiritually abused Christians know only too well how Margaret feels.

I read not long ago about ten people at a religious festival who drowned in Tanzania's Lake Victoria. Why? The article said they were trying "to walk on water like Jesus . . . as a test of faith."[11] It strikes me that far more often, sincere believers try to *heal* (themselves or others) like Jesus as a proof of their faith. The potential results can be equally as tragic.

Most conservative, evangelical Christians would scoff at word-of-faith teachings that lead to such religious extremes. Yet we often seem to believe and live something remarkably similar.

ILLUSIONS OF CONTROL IN CONSERVATIVE CHRISTIANITY

Oh, we don't try to create "millionaire status" or physical healing by the force of our faith. We just try to create or maintain favor with God by the "rightness" of our lives. Both these expressions of spiritual grandiosity distort the Gospel with control fantasy lies. But the second lie has the potential to wreak far more spiritual devastation than the first. For it mocks the gift of God's grace.

All-Grace Theology: Relinquishing Spiritual Control

Scripture declares that, as a contemporary hymn says, "Only by grace do we enter. Only by grace do we stand." (See for example, Titus 3:5-7; Ephesians 2:8-9; Colossians 2:6, for Scripture specifically addressing those two critical truths.) This means that from start to finish, our salvation and right standing with God rest on *Jesus'* perfect performance, not *ours.*

You'd think that all Christians in every church would eagerly embrace an all-grace position, wouldn't you? But, they don't.

This all-grace theology isn't easy for us overcontrollers to swallow. We're apt to choke on the need to admit our utter, ongoing inability to do *anything* good enough to merit God's favor. It's very difficult for many of us to accept the truth that all our evangelical do-gooding doesn't control God's opinion of us. That kind of thing sure worked with our folks when we were kids. And all of our friends at church seem very impressed with our Christlike deeds..

What's really confusing is that some of us who live this created-rightness lie genuinely believe in grace.

Some-Grace Theology and Illusions of Control[12]

Grace. That's a familiar word to nearly everyone in the Western world. Even confirmed pagans likely know the words to the first verse of "Amazing Grace." And we Christians hear about being "saved by grace" in our churches almost every Sunday. Goodness knows we read a lot about grace in the New Testament, especially in Paul's letters to various churches. And it's in Paul's letter to the Galatian Christians that we read about the magical-thinking and spiritual control fantasies underlying what I call some-grace theology.

In Galatians 1:6 Paul expressed his astonishment that those believers were deserting Christ and His grace. He pointed out that the Galatians had begun their Christian lives relying totally upon grace as their sole basis of being rightly related to God. But later some of them had fallen away from that very grace. (See Galatians 5:4.) In contrast, Paul explicitly stated that he had *not* set aside God's grace and substituted his own law-keeping good works as his source of righteousness. (See Galatians 2:21.) What's more, Paul implied that if we can be right with God through our own law-keeping works, then Jesus' death was a disastrous, divine blunder.

The Galatians' some-Grace theology implies that we begin our Christian lives completely dependent upon *Christ's* righteousness. However, over time that dependence decreases as we develop more and more righteousness of our own as a result of our increasingly successful law-keeping. In effect, we switch from *receiving* God's grace to *performing* good-enough works.

That last part certainly has a familiar ring to it, doesn't it? It's just magical thinking's familiar refrain transposed to the strains of "Amazing Grace." With apologies to John Newton, here's how I think it might sound. (Feel free to sing along.)

> Amazing grace, how strange the thought
> that God saved even me.
> I once knew 'twas gift, but now think I ought
> to earn grace God makes free.

Don't you think my version matches the Galatians' teachings more closely than Newton's original? Sadly, it also expresses the message conveyed by twentieth-century some-grace churches.

Control Fantasies in Some-grace Churches

Some churches almost seem to *fear* the all-grace truth about our favor with God being based solely on trusting in Jesus' righteousness from beginning to end. I wonder if they think that such amazingly good news might tempt us to cancel our church memberships, burn our Bibles, and become a pack of howling hedonists? They don't seem to trust God to put His law within His children by, as He says in Jeremiah 31:33, writing it on their hearts.

Whatever their reasons, these some-grace churches don't want to take that chance. So they set up spiritual standards to keep us living and looking like "good Christians." Obviously to make this plan work, these standards must focus on observable, public behaviors, despite the fact that who we are in the privacy of our own hearts and homes more accurately reflects our true spiritual conditions. By looking at (or hearing about) our behavior, church leaders, all of whom have already been judged to be *very* "good Christians," can determine how well those of us in the pews meet the standards. Then they can correct us when we miss the mark and reward us, usually with leadership positions of some kind, when we hit it.

The standards always forbid activities clearly condemned in the Bible such as lying, stealing, committing adultery, and not praying or meeting regularly with other believers. Curiously, I've observed that many of these churches rarely mention other clearly condemned behaviors like gluttony, gossiping, seeking power in the church, and failing to give to the poor. In addition, nearly all some-grace standards forbid behaviors *not* specifically condemned in Scripture. Some of these extra-biblical "forbiddens" include:

- *Smoking*;
- *Drinking alcohol,* or—in many cases, eating in restaurants or going to bowling alleys that serve alcohol because if other church members see us coming out of that restaurant or bowling alley, they might think we drank alcohol while we were there and that would make them start drinking alcohol;
- *Dancing,* in most cases including "minimal contact" dancing like tap, ballet, and square dancing;

- *Attending movies,* including G-rated movies because if other church members see us coming out of a G-rated movie, they might think we also attend X-rated movies and that would make them start attending X-rated movies; (the same logic may be applied to *watching television* because if people know we subscribe to the Disney Channel, they might think we have the Playboy Channel and that would make them . . . you know the rest).

Many of you know, only too well, that this represents but a few of the possible behaviors some-grace churches condemn for "good Christians." I hope you also know that I'm not advocating all the aforementioned activities for Christians, or anyone else for that matter.

The Some-grace Focus on Externals

The critical issue here is that these "forbiddens" reflect the emphasis some-grace churches put on *externals.* To be sure, these fellowships teach that we are *made* right with God by grace. But they also seem to say that we *stay right* and, in effect, *get "righter" and "righter"* the more of those (and similar) activities we avoid.

I've begun to suspect this is an attempt to create the illusion that those who adhere to the some-grace, extra-biblical standards have become not just *"good* Christians" but, *"better* Christians." It's one thing to create the illusion that we can do or not do enough to become spiritual supermen and superwomen to control our spiritual standing with other *believers.* But it's a quantum leap of grandiosity to buy into the illusion that any of those externals help us control our right relationship with *God!* Listen to pastor Craig Barnes on this subject.

Many labor under intense guilt because they cannot live up to all the standards that define "a good Christian." Rather than having a devotional life that flows out of an enthusiastic response to God's grace, large numbers of Christians are slavishly trying to arise early in the morning to get through a regimen of Scripture readings and prayers before rushing off to the real life of the office, the school, or the home. Not only is this in effect an effort to buy God's blessing for the day, but it also implies an unfortunate dichotomy between the spiritual life and the real world. . . . Time for a devotional is vitally important if it comes out of the heartfelt longing to bring our world under the umbrella of God's presence. Sadly, we tend to get that turned around, thinking that if we just do these things, we will learn how to live superhuman lives. *This makes the devotional life into yet another manipulative attempt to get to God. The fact is that God has already gotten to us in Jesus Christ*[13] (emphasis added).

Now before we light the heretics' fires, let's be honest about the magnetic pull of magical-thinking theology of whatever denominational expression. Whether by the force of our faith-filled words or the rightness of our standard-conforming behavior, nearly all of us hope to exert some control over how God runs the world. Or at least *our* particular corners of the world.

In other words—we long to escape the painful reality of suffering.

SUFFERING, FAITH, AND ILLUSIONS OF CONTROL

Christians' responses to this world's undeniable suffering seems to come in two extremes: martyrdom or magic.

Oswald Chambers noted:

> To choose to suffer means that there is something wrong; to choose God's will even if it means suffering is a very different thing. No healthy saint ever chooses suffering; he chooses God's will, as Jesus did, whether it means suffering or not.[14]

We've all heard of folks with a so-called martyr complex. That's what Chambers is talking about here. And clearly, that's not a genuinely biblical attitude. God didn't give us to our friends, parents, spouses, children, etc. to die for them. He already sent Jesus to do that.

What's more, I take comfort from the fact that when our Savior faced suffering and pain, He expressed sorrow, fear of abandonment by God, and many of the deep struggles you and I have when suffering invades our lives. His Gethsemane prayer did *not* include something on the order of, "I'm so grateful that You have chosen Me to suffer for You, Lord."

In contrast to the spiritual masochists, most of us long to live in hermetically sealed bubbles that keep us safe from the pain and suffering of this sin-polluted planet. And we may have been taught, blatantly or subtly, that God provides a passport into that bubble in response to our faith. Yet that doesn't usually match the reality of our lives or the lives of other sincere believers we know. And it certainly misses the biblical truth about faith.

BIBLICAL FAITH

In a real sense, biblical faith is not some leap in the dark. Rather it is our right response to the revelation of God's character. And since we cannot please God without it, we're wise to take the subject of faith very seriously.

What must we believe to have God-pleasing faith? According to Hebrews 11:6, we must believe in the reality of God—as He reveals Himself. We discover that reality most clearly when we look at Jesus, who is God "with skin on." We must also believe that God rewards those who have faith in Him. And this is where many folks tend to get seriously selective in their Bible reading.

Many of us seem to think that earthly success is synonymous with spiritual reward. After all, if our faith pleases God, He'll fill our pockets with money and our lives with loving people and prestigious positions. Right? Perhaps we need to take a closer look at the "faith chapter" in Hebrews.

It's true, there *are* a lot of success stories in the eleventh chapter of Hebrews. For example in verse 7, we discover that Noah had faith in God and won a cruise! However, we meet other faithful believers in verses 35-39 who didn't fare so well—to put it mildly.

So, is God only *sometimes* a rewarder? This raises the critical question of why faithful believers suffer if God rewards faith. Perhaps we find a clue to understanding this distressing dilemma tucked away in the faith-driven "success stories." In Hebrews 11:10, 13, and 16 we discover a recurrent theme suggesting that *faith's ultimate reward comes in heaven, not on earth.*

That's it? Just "pie in the sky by and by"? Can't we count on any guaranteed result from our faith here and now? According to verses 2 and 39, we have the guarantee of God's approval on what we do in faith. However—as we've already seen in verses 35-39, *even when faithful believers have God's approval, He doesn't guarantee them protection from suffering.*

No guarantees — again! *This* is the reality that pierces to the heart of all our magical thinking and illusions of control. We *demand* guarantees. Many of our churches have *promised* guarantees — if we earn God's approval.

These bogus and unbiblical promises tap into our most basic human longing for assured safety and accepting love. They pander, also, to our infantile illusions that we can control life in order to satisfy those longings. The longings, illusions, and promises combine to produce a childish, fairy-tale faith.

Fairy-tale faith asserts, "God will never let me suffer if my faith is good enough." How different that sounds from the mature, pain-refined faith of Job who declared, "Though [God] slay me, yet will I trust Him!" (Job 13:15)

WHEN BELIEVERS BECOME TRUSTERS

Suffering confronts us with the disturbing truth that the God who loves us enough to die for us also allows intense, sometimes life-shattering pain of all kinds into our lives. We can look at Jesus' response to suffering people to know that God *cares deeply* about our pain, whether physical or nonphysical. But in spite of that, suffering continues unabated on this planet — much of it undeserved by the individual sufferers. And as if that weren't enough, God has the divine audacity to invite us to trust Him in spite of all the suffering!

You've probably noticed that, like most evangelicals, I frequently refer to Christians as "believers." But I wonder if we, like Job, are "though-He-slay-me" *trusters* too? Am I? Sometimes. Often my trust wavers — or even fails temporarily. Does yours?

Job-like trusters love the Giver more than His gifts. They stubbornly insist that God is good even when life isn't. And Job-like trusters cling to the conviction that God can and *really will* work all the confusing, painful, unjust, downright terrible stuff together in a way that ends up good. (Just like He did with a Cross and an empty tomb.)

I suspect that we will continue to struggle with trusting God despite our best intentions and deep commitments. We can't figure

Him out and that drives us crazy! He's not surprised by this, you know. He told us we'd never fully understand Him and His ways. Read it for yourself in Romans 11:33-36:

> Oh, the depth of the riches both of the wisdom and knowledge of God! How unsearchable are His judgments and unfathomable His ways! For who has known the mind of the LORD, or who became His counselor? Or who has first given to Him that it might be paid back to Him again? For from Him and through Him and to Him are all things. To Him be the glory forever. Amen.

There it is. The Creator refuses to explain Himself fully to His creatures. Even those He loves to death! God makes it clear that He doesn't require our advice about how to run the universe. And He doesn't owe us anything since it is impossible for us to give Him anything He needs. (The Trinity of Father, Son, and Spirit has no unmet needs.)

What's more, God declares Himself the Source, Sustainer, and Goal of all things. Now *that's* control, my friend! Then God, so to speak, puts the ball in our courts to choose a response to this truth.

The Apostle Paul, a suffering-tried and consistently true truster, responded with a burst of praise that crystallized the hopeful implications of God's control. Whoever controls takes responsibility for outcomes. So whoever controls gets either blame or credit, depending on the outcome. In the case of ultimate, transcendent, universal control, God — in effect — gets an *A+* for outcome. A truster's conclusion: *To Him be the glory forever.*

Now God invites you and me to join Paul, and countless others, by adding *Amen.*

Think about It

Using a concordance, do a word study on *grace*. As you do, write each verse in your own words. Also include personal applications of what you're learning. Here's how one counselee's journal entry looked for Ephesians 2:8:

> *God saved me by grace through faith, and even the faith is His gift to me rather than something I whipped up on my own.* It's just so amazing to me that God does all the work and all the giving. I can't even claim credit for my faith because that is a gift too. Such generosity makes me uncomfortable really. I'm just not used to it. But it also makes me want to cry and laugh and sing all at once! And I don't think I'll ever be able to say thank You enough times to the Lord.

As you study, be sure to read the verses before and after the one in which the word *grace* appears. The example above proves the value of this approach. Read Ephesians 2:8-10 to see how verse 10 balances any tendency we might have to use the gift of grace as a license for sin.

Pray about It

DEAR LORD, The words "thank You" seem so inadequate to express what's in my heart when I think about all You have given me. Please teach me how to live my gratitude in joyous obedience. AMEN

Learn More about It

When we stop to ponder the many things God has given us, we have to reflect on His forgiveness. And when we do, we're apt to notice some control fantasies waving their magic wands once again.

ELEVEN

Illusions of Control and Forgiveness

In a cemetery not far from New York City sits a headstone engraved with a single word. No date of birth or death. No flowery epitaph. There is only a name and one word.[1]

I wish I had some information about the person buried there, don't you? But then, perhaps that person told us what he considered most important about himself.

In this chapter we will look at what it means to be forgiven by God and how our everpresent illusions of control impinge upon this divine work. Then we will shift our focus to the inevitable outworking of forgiveness in our lives as we examine some of the issues involved in forgiving others. Again, we'll discover how often magical thinking's control fantasies distort the forgiving process.

CONTROL FANTASIES ABOUT
RECEIVING GOD'S FORGIVENESS

In both the Old and New Testaments we learn that God's forgiveness flows from His gracious love for us. For example, Psalm 130:7 says:

> O [My people], hope in the LORD; for with the LORD there is lovingkindness, and with Him is abundant redemption.

I substituted the words "My people" for "Israel" so you and I could more readily put ourselves into this promise. When we do, we again face the necessity of relinquishing all efforts to do or be enough to merit either God's love or His forgiveness/redemption. Just in case you, I, or Israel of old might miss this critical truth, God spells it out in Deuteronomy 7:6-7. In those verses the LORD emphasizes He "set His love" upon His people, completely unrelated to how many they were or what they had done.

In the New Testament, God has the Apostle Paul echo this concept in Romans 5:6-11. Verse eight captures the heart of this passage: *"But God demonstrates His own love toward us, in that while we were yet sinners, Christ died for us."* We just can't escape the reality that our salvation demonstrates God's gracious love, not our religious rightness. In other words, the Creator initiates the relationship with His creatures.

Now, I realize we've been over this ground before. But we seem to have difficulty keeping this Creator–creature distinction straight. And no wonder, since this is our Original Sin in which all others have their roots.

In Jesus Christ, our loving Creator forgives our primal and persistent sin of refusing to live as the God-dependent creatures He made us.

Isn't it ironic that we appropriate the freedom divine forgiveness brings only when we accept our utter dependency upon God? "Only by having a restored appreciation of our needs, and especially of our created need for God, will we ever be free from the enslaving pursuit of pretense. God has forgiven us for trying to be God, whole and complete, and has saved us from the hell of living as if we were in control."[2]

You'd think that verses like Romans 5:8 would drive a stake through the heart of our control fantasies. However, in my own faith life I've found that my control fantasies can, as it were, take a licking and keep on ticking.

FANTASIES ABOUT FORGIVENESS
FOR BELIEVERS

I heard about a man who loved practical jokes. He once picked six of his friends at random and sent each a telegram that read: "All is known, flee at once." All six left town immediately.

How would you and I respond to such a telegram, I wonder. For, not only *is* all known, all *has been* known about each of us long before we were ever born. Known by God, of course.

When we couple the truth of God choosing to set His forgiving love on us (Ephesians 1:4), with the reality of His knowing what we'll do before we do it (Psalm 139: 4), we discover an amazing thing. *No matter what we have done, we have never disappointed God!* This means that God isn't up in Heaven shaking His head, so to speak, saying, "I had no idea Sandy would do *that!* If I had, I'd never have given her the gift of faith to trust Jesus as her Savior. I am *so* disappointed. I expected so much *more* of Sandy. I'm really ashamed to have a child like her." If this sounds bizarre or heretical, think about it for a minute. Disappointment comes from unrealistic expectations — anticipating something that does not actually happen. How could an omniscient God ever have an unrealistic expectation about *anything?*

Now don't misunderstand. *Our sins deeply grieve our Lord.* He knows how much destruction and pain sin produces in our lives and in the lives of others. In addition, our sins damage our fellowship with our Heavenly Father. He doesn't kick us out of His family after we've been born into it by faith in Jesus. But God knows we won't be as eager to spend time with Him and seek His guidance when we're pursuing *our* ways instead of *His.*

Here's what this mini-theology lesson means to you and me: nothing that we have ever done, or that anyone else has ever done to us, disqualifies us from being the objects of God's gracious, forgiving love. He's always known all of whatever it is. And He's set His love upon us anyway! Now — you have to admit — that's pretty amazing.

You may be wondering what this astoundingly good news has to do with our illusions of control. Just this: many of us who acknowledge our inability to *redeem* ourselves from sin nevertheless nurture the fantasy that we can *repair* ourselves and our sins once we *are* redeemed. As if we have to protect God's feelings and reputation, we undertake do-it-yourself repair jobs that inevitably cause additional destruction.

BIBLICAL SIN-REPAIR FANTASIES

Consider King David, that man after God's own heart. Instead of immediately confessing his adultery with Bathsheba and seeking forgiveness, David tried to fix it. That led to a downward spiral of deepening deception and murder. (See 2 Samuel 11:6-27.) David eventually confessed his sin after God sent the prophet Nathan to confront him. (See 2 Samuel 12:13 and Psalm 51.) He accepted both the judgment and the forgiveness of God. And David received the clean heart and restored joy for which he prayed.

None of David's sin took God by surprise. For in 2 Samuel 7:14-15 the Lord said: "I will be a father to [David] and he will be a son to Me; when he commits iniquity, I will correct him with the rod of men . . . but My lovingkindness shall not depart from him." Did you catch it? *When* he commits iniquity—sin. Not *if*, but *when*. David never disappointed God. And David never escaped the devastating consequences his sinful choices brought upon his immediate family and the nation he led.

I suppose the New Testament story that most clearly illustrates this same reality is the parable commonly called The Prodigal Son in Luke 15:11-32. Again, we see a dearly loved son turning his back on what we might call family values. This time, the wandering son ends up in a pigpen rather than with his neighbor's wife. But he's just as out of fellowship with the father, who represents God in this parable. Rather than return home when his inheritance was spent and seek forgiveness, the son borrowed a page from *The King David Do-It-Yourself Sin-Repair Manual*. In his case, the fix-it efforts left the lad eating pig slop. Pretty disgusting thought for anybody, but especially for a Jew. Finally this son realized his only hope was returning to his father, owning up to his wrong choices and enduring the consequences.

These amazing sagas aren't complete yet. Despite David's sometimes tragic lapses of obedience, God describes him as a man "who followed Me with all his heart, to do only that which was right in My sight," in 1 Kings 14:8. And in 1 Kings 15: 5, we find this evaluation of David: "[He] did what was right in the sight of the LORD, and had not turned aside from anything that He commanded him all the days of his life, except in the case of Uriah, the Hittite [Bathsheba's husband]."

The Parable of the Prodigal suggests that the son expected a cold shoulder when he returned home. Instead, he received a warm embrace from a loving, forgiving father. What's more, the father gave this straying son several tangible tokens of his loving favor, including a lavish banquet to celebrate his repentant return.

David and the prodigal son found loving forgiveness when they abandoned their illusional self-repair efforts, confessed their sins, and turned back to the Father. Their examples illustrate the promise of forgiveness we find in 1 John 1:9, which is clearly addressed to those who have already been born into God's family by faith in Christ. And in Romans 8:1, we learn there is no condemnation awaiting God's children when they sin. Jesus bore all God's condemnation of sin at the Cross in our place. We find this gracious truth throughout the New Testament. (See 2 Corinthians 5:21 and Colossians 2:13-14.) However, this does not mean there are no consequences for our post-salvation sins. *Sin always has consequences, and they are always destructive.*

I've known of Christian parents who have taken their unmarried, pregnant daughters to get abortions as a means of, in effect, repairing the results of the girls' sexual sins. This strikes me as remarkably similar to David's fix-it plan. These appearance-preserving families tried to do "damage control," like government agencies after a nuclear accident. In less dramatic cases, many of us throw ourselves furiously into more and more church activities in an attempt to distract ourselves and others from some sinful relationship or practice that we're not willing to acknowledge and give up. The common fantasy seems to be that it's better to create the illusion that it never happened. Or, if that fails, that what happened was no big deal.

In contrast, God asks His children to surrender all illusions of controlling, hiding, minimizing, cleaning-up, repairing, or fixing sin. He invites us to *confess* our sins instead, literally to agree with God by saying the same thing He says about sin. And as we've already discovered, God says we can't do anything except receive as a gift what He has done for us in Jesus. Of course after we have dealt with the sins that distanced us from the Lord, we can ask Him for wisdom and power to avoid repeating them.

ILLUSIONS OF CONTROLLING WITH SELF-PUNISHMENT

I once read about President Andrew Jackson pardoning a man who had been condemned to death for robbing a stagecoach. To everyone's dismay, the convicted robber refused the presidential pardon. This case eventually reached the United States Supreme Court. Here is a portion of the Court's final opinion: "A pardon is an act of grace . . . a deed, to the validity of which delivery is essential, and delivery is not complete without acceptance."[3]

The man was hung.

Like this robber, all of us who have asked Jesus to be Savior and Lord of our lives have been forgiven, pardoned from the penalty of sin. But like the convicted man, we must *accept* the gift of forgiveness/pardon to experience the freedom it brings. Frequently, our control fantasies get in the way.

Some of us may use self-punishing guilt in an illusional attempt to control and improve our behavior. We seem to believe that our own control efforts are more effective than the guiding, convicting work of the Holy Spirit in our hearts. We tell ourselves something like this: "I won't sin that way again if I stay focused on my guilt and continue to punish myself often enough." Of course, we seldom actually recognize such blatantly unbiblical beliefs and thoughts. We just live them. Like Marcia did.

"But you don't understand. . . ." Marcia's words were swept away by a wave of body-wrenching sobs as she buried her face in her hands. Marcia, whom I'd been seeing in counseling, was trying very hard to make me understand why she wouldn't let herself "feel" God's forgiveness. But her sorrow and self-loathing repeatedly reduced her to tear-choked silence. "What I haven't made clear is that" — her voice broke again as she struggled to hold back her tears — "I was a Christian when all this happened."

Marcia was referring to several years of promiscuity that began in college and included an affair with her married boss. Hungry for loving relationships, Marcia had settled for empty sex. Marcia's sexual sins haunted her.

She was determined to avoid further promiscuity. As a result, Marcia changed jobs so she could work independently out of her home. She also dropped her health club membership and gained twenty-five pounds. Marcia eventually became so depressed that she sought counseling through her church.

As Marcia replayed her record of sexual sin for me in one of our sessions, she repeatedly said: "I've confessed and confessed my sin, but I still feel so disgustingly dirty when I'm at church with other

Christians. And I can't really talk to God about anything else besides begging for forgiveness over and over."

I asked Marcia to read 1 John 1:9 from the large Bible she always brought to counseling. "Oh, I don't need to look it up, I know it by heart. 'If we confess our sins, He is faithful and righteous to forgive us our sins and to cleanse us from all unrighteousness,' " she said quickly in a singsong way. After affirming her knowledge of Scripture, I told Marcia I wasn't sure she had really done what that verse told her to do. "But, I've done it over and over. I've done it right here in the counseling office," she replied incredulously.

"But have you really said the same thing *God* says about your confessed sins—that they are forgiven and no longer an issue with Him?" Marcia's eyes welled with tears. She whispered, "I want to be able to do that more than anything." I invited her to begin asking God to bring that about in her heart. And for the first time in a very long time, Marcia talked to her Savior about something other than her past, repeatedly confessed sexual sins.

As ongoing "homework," I asked Marcia to get a concordance so she could do a Bible study on forgiveness. She also found helpful books on the topic in her Christian bookstore. Slowly, hesitantly, Marcia began to let the freedom of God's gracious forgiveness seep through her illusions of control and into her heart. In time, she was able to surrender most of the isolation and self-hatred she'd depended upon to change/control her behavior.

As Marcia's relationship with God changed, so did her attitude toward herself and others. She began attending a single adults' Bible study, and joined the church choir she'd felt "unworthy" of previously. And she also began to learn how to build healthier relationships with men.

When we believers take Marcia's magical-thinking route, we stay so fixed on what *we* have done, we virtually ignore what *Christ* has done *for* us. Without a shift of focus from *our sins* to *God's grace,* the freedom and joy of being the Father's forgiven children will remain only the stuff of ancient kings and parables. And that's a problem since only the forgiven can truly forgive.

According to verses like Ephesians 4:32, God wants those of us who have *experienced* His forgiveness to *extend* His forgiveness to others. When we attempt to follow this divine mandate, we're apt to run head-on into more of our illusions of control.

CONTROL FANTASIES ABOUT FORGIVING OTHERS

I've learned a lot about forgiving in the past few years, both as a sometimes reluctant forgiver and as a counselor to other struggling forgivers. One of the first things I learned was how many misconceptions I and a lot of other Christians have about what forgiving others is and does. Many of these common misconceptions spring from our control fantasies. Because we always fare best when we're rooted in reality, let's examine three of these control-related illusions about what forgiving others really is.

Forgiving Fantasy #1: No More Tears

In chapter 4 I talked about the fallacy of expecting ourselves to develop selective amnesia in order to "forgive and forget." Yet this is exactly what many sincere forgivers *hope* to do. In a sense, we want forgiving someone to magically make all the distressing emotions associated with a painful memory disappear. And many times, we hope to eliminate the memory itself so we can pretend it never happened.

Certainly, the quality of our painful memories usually changes dramatically after we've worked through the process of forgiving. But, in my opinion, that process has three steps: (1) face it; (2) feel it; and (3) forgive it. Too many times, we want to leap the first two steps, hoping the third will magically eliminate the need for them. I believe that forgiving is an indispensable part of the emotional and relational healing process. But it isn't a substitute for it. Neither is it a magic wand to make memories and emotions disappear.

I once counseled with a lovely Christian homemaker in her late thirties. During the time we worked together, Joanne's father had a stroke that complicated existing health problems. Even though she had, as she put it, "never felt really close" to her father, she visited him daily in the last weeks of his life.

During that time she came into a counseling session looking puzzled. She explained, "The strangest thing has happened almost every time I've seen my dad this week. He keeps asking me to forgive him, but he doesn't say for what. I say, 'Dad, there's nothing to forgive.' But then he looks more anxious and asks again. So I tell him, 'Dad, I forgive you. I forgive you.' " And Joanne sincerely meant it.

However, it was only after her father's death that Joanne understood her father's anxious deathbed pleading for pardon. That's when memories of sexual abuse began to surface. And Joanne's sincere but naive forgiving did not eliminate the need to face and feel the overwhelming terror of her incest.

Wounds take time to heal. And when the wounds are sexual, emotional, and/or relational, they require a season of recovering and healing *even when the wounding one has genuinely repented and the wounded one has sincerely forgiven.* We need to remember this whether we are the wounder*s* or the wound*ed*. Neither receiving nor extending forgiveness between individuals can make this reality magically disappear.

What's more, deep relational wounds of trust betrayal (as in affairs, spouse battering, and child abuse) may require a *very* long time to heal significantly. Appropriate trust takes time to develop in new relationships. And in existing relationships where trust has been broken, the restoration process will likely take more time than the initial trust building.

In my opinion being trusted is a privilege one earns by being consistently trustworthy. It is not an inalienable right of authority figures — even parents. In many cases of hands-on child abuse, even truly repentant parents may have to live with the tragic truth that when they repeatedly betrayed the tender trust of their helpless children, they forfeited the privilege of being trusted by them again. As we've learned, even *forgiven* sins have consequences.

This means that if you are one of these repentant parents, don't be too surprised if your adult offspring refuse to let their young children visit you alone. If Joanne had remembered being sexually abused by her father before his death, I would have supported fully her decision never to let her young children be alone with him.

Forgiving Fantasy #2: No More Protection

At this very moment, some of us may be dragging through life in the armor of unforgiveness. We believe we can control our safety by using our ancient anger and overripe resentment as shields to protect us from being hurt again by the one(s) who've hurt us before. Like all the control promised by magical thinking, our protection is an illusion.

When we need or want to continue contact with those who've hurt us (like bosses, spouses, or parents), we usually wear our unforgiveness armor *inside* our skin, so to speak. By maintaining this inner arsenal, we keep those individuals at a safe-feeling distance no matter how outwardly close the relationship may appear. In effect, we smile outside and seethe inside.

This unforgiveness can make us feel stronger, less vulnerable, safer. Besides, it may just feel good to withhold forgiveness from those important people in our lives who have withheld what we wanted from them. This can seem like a safe and "acceptable" way of hurting them. The crazy part about this, of course, is that they may never *know* we resent them. Worse yet for our infantile control illusions, even if they know, they may not *care!* Meanwhile we're hurting ourselves physically, spiritually, and nearly every other imaginable way.

Recent research suggests that when asked to recall an event that made them angry, cardiac patients experienced a change in their hearts' pumping capacities. This measurement dropped by 5 percent, meaning less oxygen-rich blood reached the tissues where it's needed. Since the patients were recalling something from the *past* that made them angry, researchers concluded that carrying bitter baggage around could be burdening our hearts.[4]

Certainly, we know that we harm ourselves spiritually when we settle for entrenched unforgiveness in response to significant hurts. In Luke 17:3, God tells us to forgive others who repent of their sins against us. And while someone's sincere admission of wrong doesn't wipe away all the pain they may have caused us, it certainly seems to help us be willing to forgive them.

However, this "if they repent" requirement is the exception, not the rule when God the Father and God the Son instruct us to forgive. In most passages, forgiving others is connected to having been forgiven. For example, in Ephesians 4:32 we're told to forgive others as God has forgiven us. And that's no easy task even for believers who cherish fantasies of being able to control just about everything all by themselves.

Forgiving Fantasy #3: No Help Needed

In recent years, many secular helping professionals, from physicians to counselors, have extolled the therapeutic benefits of forgiving. However, I seriously doubt that anyone can genuinely forgive profoundly unjust hurts apart from the working of God in their hearts.

In Mark 11:20-25, Jesus was teaching His disciples about faith as they walked together near Jerusalem. Our Savior tells them to have faith in God. Then He tells them that their faith can: (1) "move mountains"; (2) bring answered prayer; and (3) enable them to forgive so that unforgiveness doesn't hinder their relationship with their Heavenly Father. Now I realize we do not build an entire doctrine of forgiveness on one verse. Nevertheless I don't think Jesus threw in His words about forgiving others in His lesson on faith just to make the print come out even on that page of our Bibles!

I believe Christians tend to overlook the fact that extending forgiveness to others is ultimately as much an act of faith as receiving it from God. We cannot forgive others on our own (despite our best controlling efforts) any more than we can redeem ourselves. Yet in both situations, we must be willing to open our hearts and lives to receive what God wants to do in and through us. I've known many believers who have experienced this reality. One of them is a dear friend of mine I'll call Sally.

Sally is a very bright, very committed Christian working for a large Christian college. Sally loves Jesus, quotes the Bible, and knows what it means to forgive. You see, a few years ago Sally discovered that the Christian dad she idolized had been having an affair with a family friend and business associate for many years. She began to see how her father had deceived, exploited, and betrayed the trust of his wife and children. Eventually both families were destroyed. I'll let Sally tell you the rest.

> I knew I was supposed to forgive my dad. So I decided one day during my devotions that I forgave him. I sort of willed it to happen. The only problem was, it didn't. I still hated him and wanted to make him suffer as much as he'd made me and my family suffer. Next I decided I'd act in faith as if I'd forgiven him. So I started doing kind things, "turning-the-other-cheek," non-confrontive stuff even when he was being a jerk. I kept waiting for some magical breakthrough, but I only felt like a total hypocrite. And I just got more and more bitter. My prayer life was dead, I mean just going through the motions.
>
> Finally, I just gave up trying to "fake-it-until-you-make-it." At a staff retreat I sobbed my heart out to God. I said, "I *can't* for-

give him. And as You well know, Lord, I *don't* really forgive him. But, Lord, I know that You can and You do. Please work in my heart to make me a forgiver too."

Sally told me that almost imperceptibly God began to change her attitude toward her dad. Her bitterness and hatred started to seep away. She began to see her dad as the weak, sin-enslaved man he actually is. At the same time, Sally started to "speak the truth in love" to her father about how his sinful choices had hurt her. As I write this, Sally says she is still learning about how to cooperate with the Spirit of God as He gives her the power to forgive her dad and others.

My friend Sally opened her heart to God by faith and asked Him to make her a forgiver. He did. And I can add my testimony to Sally's, since God has moved mountains of bitterness in my heart to make room for forgiveness toward my mother. And even toward the father who wanted to kill me before I was born. But this doesn't mean that Sally and I and all other still-learning forgivers no longer struggle with illusions of control. I mean, after all, sincere forgivers have relinquished the right to hurt those who have hurt us, and that ought to enable us to create some major changes in our relationships. Right?

FORGIVING AND ILLUSIONS OF RELATIONAL CONTROL

Choosing to forgive does not magically change or control people's attitudes and behaviors. How I wish it did! Believing and living as if it does puts us back in Fantasyland — fast.

We may hope that if we proclaim our forgiveness, the people who hurt us will be smitten to the heart with their sins and fall on their faces before God in contrite repentance. And of course, this total, instantaneous change of heart will be accompanied by dramatic changes in their hurtful attitudes and behaviors. Sometimes we even entertain fantasies that the people we're forgiving will feel *indebted* to us. It's as if our obvious moral superiority, once they wake up and recognize it, will have the power to change the way they relate to us. Acting as if forgiving waves a magic wand that can transform even the lowest lowlife into a paragon of virtue and veracity has C-O-N-T-R-O-L I-L-L-U-S-I-O-N-S written all over it.

FORGIVING AND ILLUSIONS ABOUT RECONCILIATION

Did you hear the story about a woman who returned to her car in a crowded parking garage to find a note tucked under the windshield wiper. It said: "I have just smashed into the rear of your car. Several people who saw the accident are watching me. They think I'm writing down my name and address. They're wrong."

Some people just go through the motions of doing the right thing after they've done the wrong thing. And we will be strolling down a yellow brick road of illusional living if we try to manufacture reconciliation with folks who just go through the motions. You see, we can forgive even if those who've wronged us never admit it or want to change. However, *reconciliation* requires something more.

Scripture clearly teaches that we are reconciled to God when we admit the truth about our sins. If we insisted forever that we had done nothing wrong, there would be no reconciliation even though God had already provided our forgiveness through Jesus Christ. We can experience the freedom and peace of mind that genuine forgiveness brings, but we may never be reconciled with those we've forgiven. Their unrepentant refusals to acknowledge and change their wrong and wounding actions block the goal of reconciliation.

God and His forgiveness will change all those who've wronged us—if they *want* to change. We and and our forgiveness won't. However, *forgiving always changes us.* We inevitably learn to trust the Lord with more of what we've tried to control as we learn to forgive. And as forgiving stretches our faith in God, we may gain a new perspective on our painful pasts. In time, we may join Joseph of old in declaring:

"[They] meant it for evil, but God meant it for good."[5]

Think about It

Do you need to ask God to forgive you? Please do it now.

Read and personalize Psalm 130:7 by inserting your name in place of the word *Israel*.

As a Christian, have you been using 1 John 1:9 like a scriptural "spot remover" without a genuine willingness to change your wrong attitudes/behavior? According to Scripture, what needs to change in your life? (Remember: confessing sin is no substitute for forsaking it.)

Whose name comes to mind first when you think about the need to forgive others?

How have you been using resentment/unforgiveness as a shield against being hurt by this person again?

Are you willing, as an act of faith, to open yourself to God's Spirit to enable you to forgive that person and others? If so, tell God that now. If not, why not?

Pray about It

DEAR LORD, Thank You for the gift of forgiveness and for creating in me a clean heart. Please give me the faith to believe that You can also create in me a forgiving heart toward that person who just came to mind. AMEN

Learn More about It

We've nearly finished our journey toward recognizing and relinquishing our illusions of control. But we have one more very important stop to make. The *most* important really.

TWELVE

Illusions of Control versus the Reality of Hope

Look closely at these letters: GODISNOWHERE.

What do the letters spell? They can say *God is nowhere*.

Throughout the previous chapters, we've seen many ways in which we Christian overcontrollers live, for all practical purposes, as if *God is nowhere*. He continually seems to ignore our suggestions — even downright demands — about how to run the universe. Consequently, we have focused on trying to control those chunks of the universe that touch us and those we love. After all, when we don't sense ourselves in control of the world around us, we feel disturbingly helpless. And the more difficult our past and present lives have been and are, the more that dreaded helplessness can turn to deadly hopelessness.

Not long ago an elderly man in Detroit was diagnosed with Lyme disease.[1] Not really understanding the condition, and too frightened to ask, he became overwhelmed with grief and guilt. You see, he believed his disease was fatal and that he had passed it on to his wife of many years. And he saw no hope for either of them. He explained all this in the note he wrote just before killing his wife and himself.

What a tragedy! Lyme disease is not contagious. And it isn't fatal. But having no hope can be.

In this closing chapter we will discover that God gives His children the gift of "living hope" to replace the deadly fears that fuel our illusions of control. But many of us have the wrong idea about hope because we take our definitions from the dictionary. To appreciate the true nature of God-given hope, we must let His Word define it for us.

UNDERSTANDING BIBLICAL HOPE

Typically, we use the word *hope* to mean a vague anticipation of something pleasant. It has a kind of "Gee whiz, I sure hope so" quality not far removed from "I wish upon a star."

In starkest contrast, both the Old and New Testament describe hope as a confident, sure expectation of God's saving actions on behalf of His people.[2] Not the slightest shadow of dread or vague wishing dims the biblical concept of hope. True, biblical hope has a distinctly "not-yet" aspect to it. But that in no way weakens the guarantee of God's certain saving actions. Many of us have learned of this personally in times of deepest despair. These individual snippets of realized hope provide a sort of sneak preview for what God has in store for His whole sin-despairing creation.

Of course, as with all of God's gifts, we must reach in faith to receive this sure-but-not-yet hope. And that can be a pretty scary stretch for overcontrollers. It reminds me of watching the trapeze act high above a circus.

I'm always amazed to see the strong, daring trapeze artists standing on tiny platforms or hanging from slender lengths of metal as someone swings a trapeze bar toward them. To get the feel of this hope business, let's put ourselves in their places (with some variations.)

"Here it comes," we hear someone call to us. But in the distressingly dim light, our vision is unclear. And we would have to trust that what we see coming closer is a trapeze bar. "Reach out for it," the strong voice encourages. So we do. But then, to our horror, we recognize that we can't quite grasp it without *first* leaving our present perch or letting go of what we've been clutching! To make matters worse, a closer look reveals a major problem with where we perch and what we clutch to provide safety. They are illusions that don't actually exist!

I think that we spend our faith lives and our changing journeys in that breath-catching, midair stretch of trembly trust. The strong voice of our Savior encourages us to let go of the illusions of control we've depended on to keep us safe. He swings a cross-shaped trapeze bar our way and bids us grasp its solid-though-not-seen hope to get us across the severe circus of our Earthly existence.

Our loving Father knows we will need that cruciform hope as

we learn to face reality without the magical illusions we've used to fuzz the sharp edges of unwelcomed truths. Let's look at three aspects of the assured hope God provides to get us across the scarey spaces of our worst fears.

HOPE THAT WE'RE NEVER TOO HUMAN

Evangelical Christianity is a theology of human weakness, not human strength. Jesus went so far as to say that unless we come as little children, we might as well stay home! In comparison to their parents, children are weak, needy, easily confused. Children need constant care and frequent rescue.

Jesus could have presented God to us in any number of roles or titles that would have forged the relational template for interactions between deity and humanity. Jesus called God Father. And He taught His followers to call God Father. Why not Emperor, Creator, Highest Judge? I'm not sure, of course. But I think Jesus taught us to call God Father because adult believers need the assurance (another name for biblical hope) that we never outgrow the limitations of humanity and our childlike dependence on our Heavenly Father. Pastor Craig Barnes tells a delightful story that captures this truth.

> When my daughter Lyndsey was in first grade, she was asked to be one of the angels in our church's Christmas pageant. She and her mother spent weeks designing the most angelic costume they could imagine. Finally the big day came. After she dressed, she came bounding downstairs in her white dress, wings and halo, crying out, "Guess who Daddy! Guess who!" Beneath the long, flowing white robe protruded her pink sneakers, begrimed by all the long days she had spent playing. . . .
>
> Those little sneakers marked the real child beneath the costume. It doesn't really matter how we dress life up, or how angelic we try to appear to those around us; the signs of our humanity are always sticking out in some way.[3]

No matter how much we "mature" spiritually, we need solid hope that it's OK with God for us to be what we will always be: weak, needy children, begrimed by our sin and our world. As such we forever require our Father's protection, guidance, and power. To make this hope clear, God's Word repeatedly connects hope and salvation. Neither depends on us reaching some spiritual pinnacle since both come through grace. So we read in Colossians 1:27 that our "hope of glory" rests solely on the redeeming relationship of "Christ in [us]." And 1 Peter 1: 3 really spells it out by assuring us that we have been "born again to a living hope."

Until we let God love us, as needy and weak and sin-begrimed as He knows us to be, we will continue to wear grandiose illusions of control like angel costumes designed to hide the pink-sneakered truth of our humanity.

For the past year or so, I've "heard" God whispering, *"Stay real and hang on to Jesus."* And to a great extent, that's become my message to others. Remembering that our hope is anchored in grace and not our own "maturity" helps us do both those things. At the same time, the Holy Spirit uses this gracious assurance to repeatedly rekindle our determination to cooperate with His transforming work in us. We see evidence of our grace-inspired cooperation when we make and live more genuinely biblical choices.

But what about the areas of our lives where we've already made clearly *un*biblical choices?

HOPE THAT WE'RE NEVER TOO FAR GONE

Have you read the Gospel according to Jonah lately? That's what I call the small Old Testament book of Jonah because it contains the Good News in my favorite Bible verse. It also provides the divine assurance that God doesn't run from us even when we run from Him.

You remember the story. Jonah booked a last-minute sea cruise in an attempt to control his life and the fate of people he despised. He didn't just ignore God's direction; Jonah ran the opposite way. But God had a whale of a surprise waiting for him.

While Jonah might not have been the smartest prophet around, he certainly seemed to have a keen grasp of the obvious. Namely, when one finds oneself in the belly of a huge fish, one needs help! So Jonah reached for the God he had run from earlier. As he did, Jonah, in effect, grabbed that trapeze bar of sure-but-not-yet hope by declaring, "Salvation is from the Lord." (See Jonah 2:9.) And the next thing he knew, Jonah was puked onto shore as a result of that fish's industrial-strength indigestion.

Then comes my favorite Bible verse: *Now the word of the Lord came to Jonah the second time* (Jonah 3:1).

Oh how I love that verse! I desperately need a God of second times. Don't you? Perhaps, like me, you've misunderstood or messed-up a lot of His first-time instructions. Isn't it encouraging to know that God doesn't discard us when we do that? Instead, He brings His people His Word the second time and the two-hundredth time if needed. And each time God brings His Word to us, He brings the sure hope that we are never too far gone. For with Him there are no "lost causes" or "dead ends."

This aspect of hope is so important, God plasters it from one end of Scripture to the other in words and pictures. "Wherever, humanly speaking, the future seemed a dead end, prophets of judgment like Hosea, Jeremiah and Ezekiel opened up the divine perspective of a new beginning."[4] For example in Jeremiah 29:11, God promised a "future and a hope" to the rebellious people He had disciplined with Babylonian captivity.

Christ's crucifixion paints the most vivid portrait of never-too-late hope. "Good Friday" appeared anything *but* good on Friday. It was more like the ultimate dead end. Only the truth of Easter Sunday enables Christians to call the day of Jesus' death "good."

Some of us may feel as if all our capacity for hope already died at the hands of others and/or from self-inflicted wounds. Either way, we see only personal failure and spiritual defeat.

I once read that when news of the Battle of Waterloo was first received in England, it was brought to the south coast by ship and then sent on by semaphore signals. The message came through: "Wellington defeated," and then heavy fog rolled in and concealed the signal flags. This news of defeat spread despair throughout the nation, but when the fog lifted, the signals resumed. The completed message said: *Wellington defeated the enemy.*

Jonah certainly looked defeated in his underwater prison. God's people in Babylon appeared equally washed-up, so to speak. And a dead Messiah seemed the ultimate embodiment of crushing defeat. Yet you and I know that, despite how they looked, appeared, and seemed, none of these scenes represent defeat when we consider the more complete story.

For us, the challenge comes from the fact that we do not yet see the more complete story of our lives. Instead, we struggle to cling to the sure hope that God swings our way with the good news of second times, new beginnings, and an empty tomb.

Have you ever felt like such a lost cause that you fell into a "ditch of hopelessness," so to speak? And then you homesteaded there? I know someone who did.

Belinda's pretty face rarely wore a smile when I first met her. Her dark eyes looked weary from tearless weeping. Oh, Belinda loved Jesus, and she knew He loved her. But her three-and-a-half decades of living with repeated betrayals of trust had deadened her capacity to experience that love. And she was no longer willing to settle for that. So Belinda started to pray specifically for God to heal her.

Very slowly, Belinda began to risk connecting with other Christians who were also struggling to grow spiritually and relationally. Many of them participated in the Christ-centered growth group Belinda joined at her church. Here is part of a note Belinda wrote to me. In it she refers to an article she had shared in the group. It told about a woman who restored a dirty, defaced rag doll she named Hope. (The italicized words were underlined by Belinda.)

> Remember the Rag Doll I described in group, that I felt like? I feel like the Lord *has* picked me up out of the ditch of hopelessness. Oh, it'll take time for the cleanup and mending, but after He's done with me, I'm sure I'll be surprised at what He originally planned me to be like! Right now, I'm just happy knowing I'm resting in His arms. Of course, some days I feel like I'm slipping out of His reach, but when I'm still and listen to Him, He reassures me I belong to Him and *no one* can take me out of His Hands!

Belinda is discovering that God never considers His children too far gone to be restored. When we reach out to Him, He lifts us out of hopelessness and enfolds us with the assurance of His unfailing love. And that reality becomes the basis of our ultimate hope.

HOPE THAT WON'T DISAPPOINT

Because the Heavenly Father knows our fears of being disappointed, He promises a hope that won't disappoint. Romans 5:1-11 shines with the incandescent illumination of God's character and purposes in Jesus Christ. And in the midst of this blinding revelation we glimpse the bedrock of our living hope.

> *Therefore, since we have been justified through faith, we have peace with God through our Lord Jesus Christ, through whom we have gained access by faith into this grace in which we now stand. And we rejoice in the hope of the glory of God. . . . And hope does not disappoint us, because God has poured out His love into our hearts by the Holy Spirit, whom He has given us (Romans 5:1-3, 5, NIV).*

Many of us have been disappointed so many times. By caregivers who didn't really care, or didn't care wisely. By friends who broke our confidences and our hearts. By elected officials who wasted our money and our trust. Despite everything within and around us that mocks the possibility, God promises us a hope that won't disappoint. And He ties this sure-but-not-yet hope He gives to what He has done and who we know Him to be in Christ. So our confidence, ultimately, is not in the promise as much as it is in the demonstrated character and faithfulness of God Himself.

GOD WITH US, OUR ULTIMATE HOPE

Again, look closely at these letters: GODISNOWHERE.

Do they spell *God is nowhere* for you? Or perhaps, *God is now here.* It all depends on how you look at it.

Our only sure and steadfast hope in the kaleidoscopic chaos of our lives is that *God is now here.* That's the astounding hope promised by ancient prophets and realized when Jesus came. He was to be called Immanuel, which means "God with us." (See Isaiah 7:14 and Matthew 1:23.)

Just imagine, God not only takes us to be with Him in that sweet by and by. He comes to be with us in this rotten here and now. It's that second promise that provides *"living* hope." We will never be the same when we let ourselves be enveloped by this reality. God who fully knows us fully loves us and is at work within our lives. God is good. And, despite all appearances to the contrary, God is in control.

Now may our Lord Jesus Christ Himself and God our Father, who has loved us and given us eternal comfort and good hope by grace, comfort and strengthen your hearts (2 Thessalonians 2:16-17).

NOTES

Introduction

1 See Ephesians 4:15.

Chapter 1: Understanding Personal Power

1 I first described this experience in *Shame-Free Parenting* (Downers Grove, Ill.: InterVarsity Press, 1992), 43–45.

Chapter 2: Prolonged Magical Thinking and Illusions of Control

1 This section is adapted from my book, *Hurt People Hurt People* (Nashville: Thomas Nelson, 1993), 64–69.

2 Deirde Donahue, "A Rebirth of Gentle Reverence," *USA Today,* Sept. 26, 1990, D1–D2. I found it very interesting that the headline atop the second page of this article read "A Revolt against Christianity."

3 C.E. Cosentino, H.F. Meyer-Bahlburg, J.L. Albert, and R. Gaines (1993). "Cross-gender Behavior and Gender Conflict in Sexually Abused Girls." *Journal of the American Academy of Child and Adolescent Psychiatry* 32: 940–47.

Chapter 3: Recognizing Illusions and Illusionists

1 Professional illusionist Danny Korem and Psychiatrist Paul Meier's book, *The Fakers* (Tarrytown, N.Y.: Fleming H. Revell, 1980), is written from a distinctly evangelical perspective to "explode the myths of the supernatural." These authors firmly believe in the two sources of super-natural power discussed in Scripture: God and Satan. They firmly reject the claims of supernatural power made by some men and women.

Also excellent and fascinating is illusionist Bob Fellows' more concise work, *Easily Fooled* (Mesa, Ariz.: Mind Matters, 1989). Although not a Christian, Fellows provides valuable information about techniques of

175

manipulation and mind control used by illusionists and cults. I ordered my copy from the Cult Awareness Network, 2421 West Pratt Blvd., Suite 1173, Chicago, IL 60645. Call (312) 267-7777 for more information.

2 Jay Cocks, "Of Dogs and Other Marvels," *Time,* 14 February 1994, 64.

3 In a May 11, 1994 article in *USA Today,* Copperfield states that his goal is "to make an island disappear" on national television.

4 Cathryn Creno, "The 'New Heaven,' " *The Arizona Republic,* 28 July 1993, E1–E2

5 USA Snapshots, "Science: Hope and Mystery," *USA Today,* 28 May 1994, A1.

6 Sharon Begley and Martha Brant, "The End of Antibiotics?" *Newsweek,* 7 March 1994, 63.

7 George Will, "Facing the Skull beneath the Skin of Life," *Newsweek,* 7 March 1994, 74.

8 Associated Press, "White Tiger Kills Keeper at Miami Zoo," *The Arizona Republic,* 7 June 1994, A3.

Chapter 4: Surrendering Our Illusions of Control

1 Francis Brown, S.R. Driver, and Charles Briggs, *A Hebrew and English Lexicon of the Old Testament* (Oxford: Clarendon Press, 1968), 457.

2 I believe that God's Word teaches a process view of sanctification whereby we are progressively transformed by the renewing of our minds (Romans 12:2). The goal of our progressive sanctification/transformation is clearly articulated in Romans 8:29 — conforming to the image of our Lord and Savior Jesus Christ. I realize that many sincere Christians differ with this progressive sanctification view.

3 Colin Brown, ed., *The New International Dictionary of New Testament Theology,* Vol. 3 (Grand Rapids, Mich.: Zondervan, 1986), 874–902.

4 Everett Harrison, "Romans," *The Expositor's Bible Commentary,* Vol. 10, Frank Gaebelin, ed. (Grand Rapids, Mich.: Zondervan, 1976), 128.

Chapter 5: Magical Fixes, Change, and Counseling

1 Toronto Globe and Mail, "Personality Drug May Rob User of Inner Self: Doctor Fears Any 'Quick Fixes,' " *The Arizona Republic,* 1 May 1994, A24

2 Marilyn Murray, M.A., is a committed evangelical, an extraordinarily skillful counselor, and my friend. Marilyn specializes in intensive therapy of not less than five days, four hours per day. With very few exceptions, she only sees adults who have a counselor or therapy group to return to after the intensive therapy. For more information, contact Marilyn at: (619) 675-1187.

Chapter 6: Illusions of Control, Shame, and Perfectionism

1 Steve Wilstein, "Fatal Fear of Fat," *The Arizona Republic,* 16 August 1994, E 1-2.

2 Ibid.

3 Joe Drape, "The Judge Told Her She Was Fat," *The Atlanta Journal/ The Atlanta Constitution,* 5 September 1993, E 16.

4 Steve Wilstein, "Fatal Fear of Fat."

5 Drape, "The Judge Told Her She Was Fat," E 16.

6 Much of this section is adapted from *Shame-Free Parenting* (Downers Grove, Ill.: InterVarsity Press, 1992), 101–02.

Chapter 7: Illusions of Control in Managing Our Emotions

1 The Associated Press, "Researchers Link Heart Disease to Hidden Psychological Troubles," *The Cincinnati Enquirer,* 16 August 1992, A-14.

2 Marilyn Elias, "Hostility, Anxiety May Hold Key to Heart Attack," *USA Today,* 15 April 1994, 1A.

3 *Journal of Women's Health,* "Abuse Victims Face Health Risks, *Ladies' Home Journal,* December 1993, 86.

4 Patrick Carnes, "Abused Children Addicted Adults," *Changes,* June 1993, 77–81.

5 Lifeline, "Alcohol Study." *USA Today,* 31 August 1993, D1.

6 See Psalm 56:3; Ephesians 4:26; 1 Thessalonians 4:13.

Chapter 8: Illusions of Control in Relationships

1 Harry Schaumburg, *False Intimacy: Understanding the Struggle of Sexual Addiction* (Colorado Springs: Navpress, 1992), 28.

2 *Released from Shame* (Downers Grove, Ill.: InterVarsity Press, 1991), 128

3 I discuss these roles in detail in chapter 3 of *Counseling Adult Children of Alcoholics,* Resources for Christian Counseling, vol. 21, ed. Gary Collins (Dallas: Word, 1989).

Chapter 9: Illusions of Control within Families

1 Knight-Ridder Tribune, " 'Family Preservation' Concept Lauded, Assailed," *The Arizona Republic,* 12 August 1994, A3.

2 Sandra D. Wilson, *Hurt People Hurt People* (Nashville: Thomas Nelson, 1993), 132.

3 The Associated Press, "Push for Cemetery Splits Vail." *The Arizona Republic,* 31 August 1994, A6.

4 Thomas Giles, "The Brave New Baby," *Christianity Today,* 16 August 1993, 34–36.

5 T. Berry Brazelton, "Milestones: How Kids Learn Who They Are," *Family Circle,* 1 February 1991, 81–84.

6 Ibid., 183–84.

7 This chart is abbreviated from one that first appeared in *Shame-free Parenting* (Downers Grove, Ill.: InterVarsity Press, 1992), 188.

8 These questions are adapted from those in Schaumburg's *False Intimacy* (Colorado Springs: Navpress, 1993), 125–26.

Chapter 10: Illusions of Control and Fairy-tale Faith

1 Hank Hanegraaff, *Christianity in Crisis* (Eugene, Ore.: Harvest House, 1993), 85. This book is rapidly becoming the major source of information and critique on Health-and-Wealth Christianity.

2 M. Craig Barnes, *Yearning* (Downers Grove, Ill.: InterVarsity Press, 1991), 39.

3 Perucci Ferraiuolo, "Christian Leaders Admonish Hinn," *Christianity Today,* 16 August 1993, 38–39.

4 Ibid.

5 Hanegraaff, *Christianity in Crisis,* 89–91.

6 Ibid., 75.

7 Craig Barnes, *Yearning,* 38.

8 William Baker, "Faith, Greed, and Heresy," *Moody Monthly,* November 1993, 46.

9 A copy of this newspaper ad appeared in *The Door,* a Christian magazine noted for its pomposity-puncturing humor. In each issue, *The Door* awards its "Green Weenie" to the "Loser of the Month" selected from articles, ads, etc. (submitted by readers) that commercialize and otherwise distort the Gospel of Jesus Christ.

10 Tom Smail, Andrew Walker, and Nigel Wright, *The Love of Power or the Power of Love* (Minneapolis: Bethany House, 1994), 80. I think these authors thoroughly and sensitively assess the problems within the Word-of-Faith movement.

11 Reuters, "Priest, 9 Pupils Drown Trying to Walk on Water," *The Arizona Republic,* 28 October 1993, A20.

12 I first discussed what I call some-grace and all-grace theology in chapter 12 of *Hurt People Hurt People* (Nashville: Thomas Nelson, 1993).

13 Barnes, *Yearning* 64.

14 Quoted in *Closer Walk* (Walk Thru the Bible) for 10 August 1993.

Chapter 11: Illusions of Control and Forgiveness

1 "Forgiven," *Closer Walk* (Walk Thru the Bible), 8 May 1993.

2 Craig Barnes, *Yearning* (Downers Grove, Ill.: InterVarsity Press, 1991), 117.

3 Michelle Lewis Starr, "A Terrible Thing to Waste," *Confident Living,* April 1991, 46–47.

4 Health Front, *Prevention*, January 1993, 11–12.

5 See Genesis 50:20.

Chapter 12:   Illusions of Control versus the Reality of Hope

1 I first told this story in the introduction to *Hurt People Hurt People* (Nashville: Thomas Nelson, 1993).

2 E. Hoffman, "Hope" in *The New International Dictionary of New Testament Theology,* Vol. 2, ed., Colin Brown (Grand Rapids, Mich.: Zondervan, 1986), 238–44.

3 Craig Barnes, *Yearning* (Downers Grove, Ill.: InterVarsity Press, 1991), 64–65.

4 E. Hoffman, "Hope," 238–44.